E. (Elizabeth) Prentiss

**How Sorrow was changed into Sympathy**

E. (Elizabeth) Prentiss

**How Sorrow was changed into Sympathy**

ISBN/EAN: 9783337119577

Printed in Europe, USA, Canada, Australia, Japan

Cover: Foto ©ninafisch / pixelio.de

More available books at **www.hansebooks.com**

# HOW SORROW WAS CHANGED INTO SYMPATHY.

## WORDS OF CHEER FOR MOTHERS

### BEREFT OF LITTLE CHILDREN.

OUT OF THE LIFE OF

MRS. PRENTISS,

*Author of the "Susy Books," etc.*

NEW YORK:
ANSON D. F. RANDOLPH & COMPANY,
900 BROADWAY. COR. 20th ST.

NEW YORK:

Edward O. Jenkins,
*Printer*,
20 North William St.

Robert Rutter,
*Binder*,
116 and 118 East 14th Street.

*This volume contains the story of Eddy and Bessie, written by* Mrs. Prentiss *shortly after their death and passages from which were given in her memoir, verses relating chiefly to the loss of these children, a few of her letters to bereaved friends, and some thoughts by the editor on the death of infants. The most of it is now printed for the first time. The work is designed specially for mothers who mourn the loss of young children. And may it please God to comfort every one of them who shall read it, with His own peace!*

*G. L. P.*

New York, *February*, 1884.

# THE DEATH OF LITTLE CHILDREN IN THE LIGHT OF FAITH.

VARIOUS estimates have been formed as to the proportion of mankind that die in infancy; some making it more than a third, others not less than one-half. Such estimates are, of course, largely guesswork. The proportion has differed at different periods and among different tribes and nations. The wide prevalence of infanticide, as in India and China, for example, has greatly increased it; and so have other criminal practices, both in heathendom and Christendom. But irrespective of such special causes, it is certain that a vast number of the human race have died, and still die, in early childhood. Little graves abound in every place of burial. There

*Infant mortality.*

are comparatively few households out of which no infant bier was ever carried. How many have been bereft of all their children! The humane spirit of modern society, aided by medical skill and sanitary science, has done much to reduce the scale of infant mortality; but it is still large enough to cast a dark shadow over the face of existence. It suggests a problem full of perplexity, and which science and philosophy seem alike unable, or unwilling, to grapple with.

*Death of infants as a natural event. Its hopelessness.* Viewed solely as a natural event, it is true, the death of little children, however grievous, is yet of a piece with the general course of the world. By no choice of their own they are thrust upon this earthly stage of being and forced to take their chance in the bitter struggle of life. It is no more strange, perhaps, that they so often succumb than that so many spring blossoms drop off and perish. Nature cares as little for young children as for young animals or plants. Nor is the death of infants at all more strange than that of boys and girls, or of young men and maidens. In either case death is full of anguish and disappointment. It is, too, so inexorable, the blow it deals is so stunning, that we have no will to resist, and can only express our amazement in groans and tears, or else in the dead silence of grief.

But if we view the death of little children on its moral side, the case is wholly altered. *The death of infants as a Providential event.* For here we have to do—not with blind chance or with inexorable physical law, but with the ruling hand of God, the Father Almighty. His providence embraces all events, both great and small, which affect human destiny. It would be as atheistic to say that without Him an infant leaves the world, as to say that without Him it came into the world. This is, indeed, a truth hard to believe, both because it lies so entirely beyond the sphere of sense, and because it is so sublime and consoling. Some things seem almost too good to be true; and this is one of them. For what is implied in our saying that the death of an infant is a Providential event? It is implied that an infant has an immortal soul and is a special object of God's care and interest. In a certain sense, to be sure, the birds of the air, the fishes of the sea, and even the lilies of the field, are objects of the Divine care. But not as spiritual beings; not as made in God's image; not as capable of knowing and loving Him and of enjoying Him forever. It is in this peculiar sense that He cares for little children. He is their Father in heaven, and His love for them is infinitely more tender than that felt by their earthly parents. On the ground of this great love rests the belief, so unspeakably comforting, that if early taken out of the world, they do not perish, but inherit everlasting life.

This belief did not always prevail. It has been the slow growth of centuries. We find nothing like it in the ethnic religions, and but little trace of it is to be found in the Old Testament. *Growth of this belief. Its connection with the birth and teaching of Christ.* The earlier revelations contain many proofs of God's gracious interest in children. The law of Jehovah protected them, and provided most carefully for their pious training. But they were regarded as members of the family and sharers in its covenant privileges rather than in their infant personality, as destined to live forever. How little there is in the Old Testament about the future existence of either parents or children! The distinct annunciation of both their immortality and its blessedness seems to have been reserved for "*the fulness of the time*" when He came, who is the light equally of this world and the next. Until Jesus said: "*Suffer the little children to come unto Me, and forbid them not, for of such is the kingdom of heaven*"; until

## X

He "*took them up in His arms, put His hands upon them and blessed them,*" infant salvation was a conjecture only—at best a hope—but not an assurance. And even the wonderful saying of the Lord Jesus would have remained an enigma, had not His own nativity furnished a key to its meaning. It may stagger the mere intellect to understand how the Babe in the manger could have been at the same time the Incarnate Word, the only-begotten of the Father; but surely no one, whose faith *does*, sincerely and in tranquil conviction, accept this amazing truth, ought to marvel at the doctrine of infant personality, or that the souls of those dying in infancy enter into life eternal.

The Incarnation shows us that Divinity itself once dwelt in a new-born child. "*And the angel said unto them, Fear not; for behold I bring you good tidings of great joy, which shall be to all people. For unto you is born this day in the city of David, a* SAVIOUR, WHICH IS CHRIST THE LORD."

And Christ is not the Saviour only, He is

also the Pattern and Ideal of our humanity in all the stages of its development; childhood no less than manhood is complete in Him alone; yea, in Him both alike have their being. *"All things have been created through Him, and unto Him; and He is before all things, and in Him all things consist."*[1] A supernatural light, issuing from His cradle, has shone upon ten thousand, yea, ten thousand times ten thousand cradles ever since. How many myriads of pious mothers have sung, and are still singing, their little ones asleep to the music of His name! The story of His advent has been the inspiration of art and of literature. Probably no other picture in all the world attracts to its shrine so many pilgrims, or adorns so many homes, as that of the Divine Child in the arms of the blessed among women.

Some of the fairest gems of poetry, too, reflect His infantile grace and loveliness. This is strikingly true in our own language.

---

[1] COLOSS. i. 16, 17.—Rev. Ver.

From Spenser to Wordsworth and Keble it abounds in Christmas carols, in lullabies and hymns of childhood, in threnodies and epitaphs, which are full of sweetness and pathos, because they are so full of Him. Here is a specimen from the "Hallelujah" of George Wither, a Puritan poet and soldier of Cromwell's time:

> When God with us was dwelling here,
>   In little babes He took delight;
> Such innocents as thou, my dear!
>   Are ever precious in His sight.
>     Sweet baby, then forbear to weep;
>     Be still, my babe; sweet baby, sleep.
>
> A little infant once was He,
>   And strength in weakness then was laid
> Upon His virgin mother's knee,
>   That power to thee might be convey'd.
>     Sweet baby, then forbear to weep;
>     Be still, my babe; sweet baby, sleep.
>
> The wants that He did then sustain,
>   Have purchased wealth, my babe, for thee;
> And by His torments and His pain,
>   Thy rest and ease securèd be.
>     My baby, then forbear to weep;
>     Be still, my babe; sweet baby, sleep.

Thou hast yet more to perfect this,
  A promise and an earnest got,
Of gaining everlasting bliss,
    Though thou, my babe, perceiv'st it not.
      Sweet baby, then forbear to weep;
      Be still, my babe; sweet baby, sleep.

A new conception of childhood, in truth, entered the world with the infant Redeemer. *New conception of childhood and of infant destiny introduced by the Gospel.* In no sphere of human life was the change wrought by His coming greater or more full of blessing. At first the change, perhaps, did not appear so distinctly as in the sphere of manhood and womanhood; but from age to age it has revealed itself with ever-increasing power. Nor can we thank God too often, or too much, that in our own day its real significance and the benedictions wrapt up in it are so clear to the eye of faith. Especially is this the case with respect to those dying in infancy. For many centuries it was a doctrine of the Church that by water baptism alone could their salvation be made sure; and in later times, the opinion widely prevailed that, whether baptized or not, only a certain elect number of them would inherit eternal life. These and various other theories limiting the salvation of infants, are still more or less widely held by good men; not, surely, from any special lack of tenderness, but because, in their view, such limitation is required by fidelity to the teaching of Scripture. The theories in question, however, no longer rule the Christian Church; to a large extent they have lost their power, and are regarded as in conflict with the real teaching and spirit of the New Testament. It is now a common belief, in the Protestant churches at least, that all infants, dying in infancy, are regenerated and saved by Christ through the Spirit. A single extract from the writings of the late Dr. Charles Hodge will suffice to indicate the change of opinion on this subject, which has taken place within our own century. His language may be too strong as to the extent of the change, but coming from so eminent a champion of the old Calvinistic orthodoxy, furnishes of itself a striking proof that the change is very great and radical:

The Scriptures teach, according to the common doctrine of Evangelical Protestants, that all who die in infancy are saved. This is inferred from what the Bible teaches of the analogy between Adam and Christ. "Therefore, as by the offence of one judgment came upon all men to condemnation, even so by the righteousness of one the free gift came upon all men unto justification of life. For as by one man's disobedience many were made sinners, so by the obedience of one shall many be made righteous" (Rom. v. 18, 19). We have no right to put any limit on these general terms, except what the Bible itself places upon them. The Scriptures nowhere exclude any class of infants, baptized or unbaptized, born in Christian or in heathen lands, of believing or unbelieving parents, from the benefits of the redemption of Christ. . . . . Not only, however, does the comparison, which the apostle makes between Adam and Christ, lead to the conclusion that as all are condemned for the sin of the one, so all are saved by the righteousness of the other, those only excepted whom the Scriptures except; but the principle assumed throughout the whole discussion teaches the same doctrine. That principle is, that it is more congenial with the nature of God to bless than to curse, to save than to destroy. If the race fell in Adam, much more shall it be restored in Christ. If death reigned by one, much more shall grace reign by one. This "much more" is repeated over and over. The Bible everywhere teaches that God delighteth not in the death of the wicked; that judgment is His strange work. It is therefore contrary, not only to the argument of the apostle, but to the whole spirit of the passage, to exclude infants from the "all" who are made alive in Christ.

The conduct and language of our Lord in reference to children are not to be regarded as matters of sentiment, or simply expressive of kindly feeling. He evidently looked upon them as the lambs of the flock for which, as the Good Shepherd, He laid down His life, and of whom He said they shall never perish, and no man could pluck them out of His hands. Of such, He tells us, is the kingdom of heaven, as though heaven was, in great measure, composed of the souls of redeemed infants.[1]

Much relating to this subject is, indeed, wrapt in mystery. It suggests many questions to which neither reason nor Scripture enables us to give a definite answer. Precisely when, or how, the souls of those

---

[1] *Syst. Theol.*, vol. i., pp. 26, 27.

dying in infancy are renewed and saved by Christ, we can not tell. But all that we willingly leave to Christ Himself and to the Blessed Comforter, by whose gracious power their salvation is wrought. Nor can we tell how, in the world within the veil, the new life, which had no opportunity for growth here, develops itself there unto the measure of the stature of the fulness of Christ. This also we gladly leave to the Master Himself,—content to know that our little ones are with Him and are "nurslings of the Holy Ghost."

In the memoir of Mrs. Prentiss occurs the following passage: *The design of this volume.*

A chapter might be written about her love for little children, the enthusiasm with which she studied all their artless ways, her delight in their beauty, and the reverence with which she regarded the mystery of their infant being. Her faith in their real, complete humanity, their susceptibility to spiritual influences, and, when called from earth, their blessed immortality in and through Christ, was very vivid; and it was untroubled by any of those distressing doubts or misgivings that are engendered by the materialistic spirit and science of the age. Contempt for them shocked her as an offence against the Holy Child Jesus, their King and Saviour. Her very look and manner as she took a young infant, especially a sick or dying infant, in her arms and gave it a loving kiss, seemed to say:

> "Sweet baby, little as thou art,
> Thou art a human whole;
> Thou hast a little human heart,
> Thou hast a deathless soul."[1]

The following pages exemplify what is here said. They show Mrs. Prentiss' tender feeling towards young children as a Christian mother; how that feeling was deepened and enriched by sorrow; and how the sorrow was transfigured into loving sympathy. In all this her case is not peculiar; it is that of thousands of Christian mothers, who have passed, or are passing now, through a like experience. The story of Eddy and Bessie is all the time repeating itself; and similar letters to bereaved

---

[1] *The Life and Letters of Elizabeth Prentiss*, p. 305.

friends every day cross each other on their errands of holy cheer and solace. *As in water face answereth to face, so the heart of man to man.* It consoles us in affliction to know that in our sighs and tears and groans we are not alone;—that others have felt just as we do; that others, too, have cried unto God *out of the depths;* and that, after they had suffered a while, He gave them *beauty for ashes, the oil of joy for mourning, the garment of praise for the spirit of heaviness.*

This little work contains nothing strange or new. The simple narrative, the verses and letters, which compose it, were penned many years ago, and without a thought that they would ever meet the eye of the public. And they would not now do so, had not the extraordinary favor with which the memoir of Mrs. Prentiss has been received, led the editor to hope that they might prove a word in season to some weary, sorrow-stricken hearts. He feels, as she so deeply felt, that no office is more Christ-like than that of a comforter; and that few so much need its gentle and cheering ministrations as mothers weeping at the graves of their children.

## I.

*Eddy's Birth and suffering Babyhood—Given back as from the Grave—"Not mine, but God's."*

Ah, joyful hearts that know not grief,
   Can never Jesus know;
He must be learned in darksome nights,
   Where bitter fountains flow;
Where souls are floated off to sea
   By tides of earthly woe.

There have I met Thee, dearest Lord;
   And oh, how passing sweet
Was to my sinking soul the sound
   Of Thine approaching feet!
To point Thee out to drowning ones,
   Oh, make me, make me meet!

## I.

OUR dear little Eddy was born at New Bedford, on Sunday, October 22, 1848, at three in the afternoon. His father was preaching at the time, on "Walking with God," and gave him his first greeting while his own heart was full of this delightful subject. We had selected for our first boy the name of Robert Leighton, and called him so for about a week, when it was exchanged for that of Edward Payson, in consideration of his having been born on the anniversary of his grandfather's death. He was a fine, healthy-looking boy, with a high forehead, dark blue eyes, and a good deal of hair on his head. On the Saturday succeeding his birth, we heard of my dear mother's serious illness; and when he was about three weeks old, of her death.

We were not surprised that his health suffered from the shock it thus received.[1] He began, at once, to be afflicted with distressing colic, which gave him no rest, day or night. We supposed he would soon

---

[1] In a letter to a kinsman, written some years later, occurs the following passage:

"Are you not all making a sad mistake in keeping C. ignorant so long of that [the sudden death of a sister] which she must learn, otherwise, on her sick-bed? Is she not in a bodily state *now* of less feebleness than she will be then; and, consequently, better able to bear this distressing news? You will say it is not to be communicated on her sick-bed; but I greatly mistake if she does not so long for her sister's congratulations on the birth of her child, that it will be necessary to explain why they are withheld. I feel strongly on this point; for my friends, through ill-judging kindness, kept me ignorant of my dear mother's illness till after the birth of my little boy; and when I was awaiting in a kind of transport of joy her sympathy in my gladness, I learned that she was on her dying bed. Eddy was just a week old, and I had no way of diverting my mind by employment of any sort— nothing to do but to lie the long day, the long night,

surmount this disorder; but on the contrary, he grew worse and worse. His father used to call him a "little martyr," and such indeed he was, for many long, tedious months.

At last, between want of sleep and pain, he was sadly worn and emaciated, and Dr. Mayhew advised the use of opiates. We ad-

---

reflecting on my sorrow. The constitution of my child received a shock from which it never recovered; and I have not a single doubt that he would now, as far as human eye can see, be living in the enjoyment of the fine health of which he gave promise, had my affliction been made known to me before his birth, when I was not tied to one spot, with an unsympathizing nurse ever present to witness my sufferings and upbraid me for them; yes, if on *my knees* I could have spread my case before God. Affliction has, in my case, come hand in hand with every child; I have left my sick-room each time in mourning garments. This makes me feel for C., as I can not describe. L. told me how much she suffered in this condition; here, too, I can feel for her as a fellow-sufferer, for not one in ten thousand knows as well as I do the worth of a child, for whose attainment the agonies of months of martyrdom must be the penalty. All this must be my excuse for venturing to question your judgment."

ministered them with reluctance, but it was only by their aid we could procure for the little sufferer the sleep he could not live without. No language can describe the scene our nursery presented month after month; during which he was never well enough for a single hour, with one exception, to be dressed and taken from the room. He wore little night-gowns till he was old enough to put on short frocks. Often, for his and my own health, we attempted to ride out, but just as the carriage would drive to the door, one of his paroxysms of pain would come on, and before we could get off his cloak, or I could throw off mine, we must hasten to administer something for his relief. A few moments' delay would reduce him to a state bordering so closely on convulsions, that I never dared wait even to deliberate what remedy I would use; something must be snatched up at once.

On the 16th of February the doctor,

who had visited him at intervals, of his own accord, came and spent about two hours carefully investigating his case. He examined Eddy particularly, and said it was a most trying condition of things, and he would gladly do something to relieve me, as he thought I had been through "enough to *kill ten men.*" He urged me to increase the nightly dose of laudanum, declaring that, in his opinion, the child was suffering severely from want of sleep. During the next two weeks Eddy became more and more feeble; he was so emaciated that if I had had any time for such indulgence of my feelings, I should have shed floods of tears whenever his little wasted frame was exposed to view. I dreaded washing and dressing him, because in this process I was obliged to see how every day he was losing flesh.

Some persons had suggested that he cried from hunger, and I had made various attempts to feed him without having courage to persevere in the face of the danger to which I knew *ill-chosen* diet must expose him. I was thus driven to procure a wet-nurse for him. A woman lived near by who had a child of about Eddy's age, plump and in fine health; I engaged her to come once in three hours to nurse him, and thought there was some reason to hope this plan might result in a favorable manner. The first day on which this experiment was tried, Eddy could with difficulty swallow a drop of the new nourishment thus provided for him; his sufferings all day were terrible; and when at night he at last fell asleep under the influence of an opiate, I could only lie and watch his uneasy slumbers, thinking he might not survive till morning. On learning what I had done, Dr. M. hastened in to remonstrate with me on what he at first deemed a rash act. But on seeing the condition the poor little creature was in, he said I had done *just right*, and that, though there was now little hope that the child could be raised to health, the season of the year was in his favor, and there was a *possibility* that before warm weather arrived, a change for the better might occur. He said if I had continued to nurse him, that mother and child would have shared one grave very speedily.[1]

For two or three days after this, Eddy declined so fast that I expected to see him breathe his last from hour to hour. I asked the nurse if she had ever seen so feeble a child; she said she had. I asked

---

[1] In a letter to her husband's mother, written at this time, she says: "I can't describe what we have suffered during the past week. But if Eddy gains strength on the new milk, he will probably get the upper hand of his trouble. His eyes are as bright as diamonds, but otherwise he does not look at all like himself. We can only wait in hope and patience. Dear mother, we are in a good school, hard as it is, and we shall not suffer one pang too many; so don't worry about us, if you can help it; will you? We long to see you, but we feel that you are very near us in your love and sympathy and prayers; and that is next best to being with you."

her if it lived, and she said, "*Oh, no!*" and afterwards told me that she thought he would die in her arms, every time she took him from mine. At the end of the first week, however, he had evidently improved; and from that time gained flesh and strength very rapidly. I now left off nursing him myself, and began to feed him, and at the end of a month, as he was quite recruited, and had an excellent appetite, and as his nurse became irregular and careless about coming, I dismissed her. He continued to thrive on the arrowroot prepared for him, though there was little, if any, improvement as to his colic. Still, he had now more strength with which to bear this pain, and we kept hoping every day he would be freed from it.

His aunt Tibby came, this spring, to help me take care of him, and he became much attached to her, as she did to him. She stayed till he was more than a year old, and devoted herself to him day and night.

When he was about eight months old, we determined to discontinue the use of opiates. He was now a fine, healthy baby, bright-eyed and beautiful, and his colic was reducing itself to certain seasons in each day, instead of occupying the whole day and night, as heretofore. We went through fire and water, almost, in trying to procure for him natural sleep. We swung him in blankets, wheeled him in little carts, walked the room with him by the hour, etc., etc.; but it was wonderful how little sleep he obtained, after all. He always looked wide awake, and as if he did not *need* sleep. His eyes had gradually become black, and when, after a day of fatigue and care with him, he would at last close them, and we would flatter ourselves that now we too should snatch a little rest, we would see them shining upon us in the most amusing manner, with an expression of content and even merriment.

About this time he was baptized. I well

remember how, in his father's study, and before taking him to church, we gave him to God. He was very good while his papa was performing the ceremony, and looked so bright and so well, that many who had never seen him in his state of feebleness, found it hard to believe he had been aught save a vigorous and healthy child. One lady told me that she laughed right out in church, because his father and he looked so alike. He is, indeed, his papa's own boy, saving the eyes.

My own health was now so broken down by long sleeplessness and fatigue, that it became necessary for me to leave home for a season. Dr. Mayhew promised to run in *every day* to see that all went well with Eddy; his aunty was more than willing to take this care upon herself, and many of our neighbors offered to go often to see him, promising to do anything for his safety and comfort, if I would only go. Not aware how miserable a state I was in,

I resolved to be absent only one week, and only took with me clothes for that week; but I was away for a whole month. As soon as I had gone, his aunt Tibby had him daguerreotyped, and sent the picture to me. It was like him, except in its being so very dark, while he was fair, and had light hair. On my return I found him looking finely. He had had an ill turn, owing to teething, which they had kept from me, but had recovered from it, and looked really beautiful.

His father and uncle S. S. had been to see him once during our vacation, and we were now expecting them again with his aunt Mary and the three children and his grandmother. We depended a great deal on seeing Eddy and Una together, as she was his *twin* cousin, and only a few hours older than he.

But the very evening of their arrival he was taken sick, and though they all saw him that night looking like himself, by the next morning he had changed sadly. He grew ill and lost flesh and strength very fast, and no remedies seemed to have the least effect on his disorder, which was induced by teething. His aunt Mary used to help us in the care of him, and would walk with him in her arms to relieve us. On Sunday, September 16th, he was very low and suffered a great deal; he would not allow us to sit with him one moment, and he was carried about the nursery day and night, during which his countenance had a strange, unnatural expression and aspect, and he constantly pressed his feet against the breast of whoever was carrying him, as if in terrible distress. His aunt Tibby and I were alone with him at night, and became more and more alarmed. At two in the morning I woke his father, told him how Eddy appeared, and asked him to go to the doctor and describe his condition. He was gone only a few moments, and on his return, said the doctor had ordered fifteen drops more laudanum; and retired again to bed, having had a hard day's work on Sunday. We gave Eddy with great reluctance this additional opiate, as he had had a good deal during the day, both by the usual mode and in starch enemas. His distress increased till we thought him dying; and his aunty ran across the street for a neighbor, who came directly. She was a person of experience, and after giving one glance at the poor little sufferer, ran herself for the doctor, though it was still dark. He came directly; was much concerned to see Eddy in such a state; said there had been a great change during the night, and that the remedies employed had acted unfavorably. I said I had thought him dying; he replied, "He is not dying *now*," but sat down with an air of despondency that made me soon after ask if I had not better call Mr. Prentiss. He said I had, and I did so.

The first dull light of morning began to

steal in and to reveal the change a single night had wrought in our dear child. The doctor still remained, and now and then took him from our arms, and himself carried him up and down the nursery, remarking that it was a wonder and a mercy that Eddy did not go into fits. As soon as it became light we sent for Miss Deborah, who was our ever-faithful friend in the time of trouble; his aunt Mary came from her room, and shortly after his grandmother Prentiss from hers. On looking at Eddy she burst into tears, and asked me if I felt willing to give him up. The doctor said there was nothing to be done, and left us; and with breaking hearts we knelt around our apparently dying child, who now lay exhausted in Miss Deborah's lap, while his father, as well as tears would let him, commended his spirit to God. The laborious respiration of the dear little one now filled the room; the intervals between being so long, that again and again I held my own breath, thinking he had gone. The doctor came in again, before long, and as Eddy now lay in my arms, I thought again that he had dropped away; but presently there came another long, weary breath to assure me he still lived. The third time the doctor came he brought a mixture of chloroform, camphor, etc., and said if the child were his own he would try this as a last resort. We made no objection to his giving it to Eddy; for myself, I did not believe anything could now save my precious baby, and had given him to God so unreservedly that I was not conscious of even a *wish* for his life.

Soon after the administration of a few drops of the mixture, however, Eddy fell asleep, and slept about five minutes, when his little cousins, who were all at play in the garden, unconscious of his situation, burst into loud shouts of laughter, which aroused him at once. But even this little repose refreshed him. He had had no sleep for a great number of hours; I think more than sixty. The doctor, on his next visit, expressed great satisfaction with this improvement; continued the chloroform, and in the course of the day, Eddy had several of these little naps, which did him good. As the day declined our hopes rose. On making his *seventh* visit in the evening, the doctor absolutely forbid my taking any more care of Eddy at night; and we left him in the kind hands of watchers, as he was so nearly unconscious as not to perceive that strangers ministered to him in his mother's place. Our chief ground of hope for many succeeding, anxious days, was the mere fact that he *lived*. We were obliged to give nourishment with the utmost caution, and to keep bottles of hot water at his feet, and to warm his little cold hands in our own. He now lay in the swinging cot, of which he had been so fond, and slept a good deal. When, at last, we saw evident tokens of returning health and strength, we felt that we received him a second time as from the grave. To me, he never seemed the same child. My darling Eddy was lost to me, and another, and *yet the same*, filled his place. I often said afterwards, that a little stranger was running about my nursery; not mine, but God's. Indeed I can not describe the peculiar feeling with which I always regarded him after this sickness, nor how the thought constantly met me, 'He is not mine; he is God's.' Every night I used to thank God for sparing him to me *one day* longer, thus truly enjoying him *a day at a time*.

## II.

*A Year old—The Cloud changed into Sunshine.*

Now let me lay the pearl away,
That on my breast I've worn all day;
How sweet, how soft the casket fair,
Where hides all night my jewel rare.

My snow-white lamb, thy gambols o'er,
Thy sportive limbs must sport no more;
Now to thy rest, let slumber creep
With gentle tread to bid thee sleep.

My winsome one! my heart's delight!
I give thee to the arms of night;
Oh, darksome night! with soft caress
My darling little baby bless.

My heart's delight! my pearl, my lamb!
How rich, how blest, how glad I am!
In sweetest sleep I see thee lie;
Good-bye, good-night! good-night, good-bye!

## II.

I HAD kept a little journal about A., and her father now wished me to begin Eddy's. On his birthday he went out to procure a book for this purpose. This is the first record:

*October* 22, 1849.—Our dear little Eddy is a year old to-day, and his papa has been out to buy this book for him. If he lives, it will be a gratification to him years hence; if he is taken from us, it will be of great comfort to us in our sorrow.

It has pleased God to make him a very great sufferer during most of his short life, and twice in the course of the year we have believed him at the point of death. He has been restored to us, we know not for what purpose; and while we thank God for this great mercy, we pray that it may prove a mercy indeed, and that we may see him grow up a "perfect man in Christ Jesus."

He is considered by many a beautiful boy; he has a very fine forehead, bright black eyes, and an uncommonly intelligent, sunshiny smile. He has been put back by his sickness, so that he is but just beginning to be interested in trying to sit alone in a little chair, and to get about, by the help of the furniture, upon his feet. But for this last sickness, he would undoubtedly have walked by this time, as previously he was always on his feet. We fancied he could say *"Eddy"* before his illness; for instance, if he dropped a toy, he would keep saying, "Eddy, Eddy!" till we returned it to him. But he never says so now. He tries very hard to say "kitty," and whenever he sees her coming cries, "Taty! Taty!" and laughs and shouts and throws his little body into all sorts of shapes. He began to shake his hand as good-bye some months ago, and is a famous kisser. In this respect, as in many others, he is unlike A. He thinks everything she does is cunning; and shouts for joy when she comes into the nursery, and when his eye first falls upon her, as he awakes from a nap. He keeps kissing her whether she likes it or not, and really hurts her by his vivacious greetings. His aunt Tibby taught him all he as yet knows. She has gone, and he misses her sadly. He has four teeth, wears high-necked, long-sleeved dresses, and though he still looks like a child who has suffered, and is delicate, no one could mistake him for a girl, he is so decidedly a *boy* in every feature and motion.

As his aunt Tibby had gone on another errand of love and mercy, to Portland, the whole care of Eddy was thrown upon me; and my health, already miserable, soon gave way. I could get very little sleep, he was so restless; he had parted with his old enemy, the colic, during his last illness; but teeth were now coming, and they kept him wakeful, though he did not appear to suffer much with them. I used to think I was out of bed with him fifty times a night. We began to think seriously of procuring a nurse for him. We had often talked of it, but I could not bear to give him up to a stranger, and we put it off from day to day till I was in such a state from loss of sleep, that I feared I should lose my senses. One evening, when I was sick in bed, his father went out and engaged Margaret, of whom we had heard excellent accounts, to come that very night.

This was the sixth of December, and without much difficulty she succeeded in attaching the dear child to her, and from that night until his last sickness, with the exception of one or two necessary interruptions, he slept with her, and took his food from her hands. He soon began to sleep with his little arms around her neck, and to repay her with his affection for the many sleepless hours he cost her. His uncle Henry and aunt Tibby came on the same night with his nurse, and his uncle said he would not go to California until he had seen Eddy walk. He was on his feet most of the time, and seemed to be restrained from running alone merely by timidity. With a little encouragement, therefore, from his uncle, he learned to walk very well. This is the next record of the journal:

*January* 5, 1850.—Eddy is now fourteen months old, has six teeth, and walks well, but with timidity. He is at times really beautiful. He is very affectionate, and will run to meet me, throw his little arms round my neck, and keep pat, pat, patting me, with delight. He tries to talk, but says nothing distinctly. Miss Arnold sent him, at New Year's, a beautiful ball, with which he is highly pleased. He rolls it about by knocking it with a stick, and will shout for joy when he sees it moving. Mrs. Allen sent him a rattle and another toy. He is crazy to give everybody something, and when he is brought down to prayers, hurries to get the Bible for his father; his little face all smiles and exultation, and his body in a quiver with emotion. He is like lightning in all his movements, and is never still for an instant. Except that his teeth trouble him, he is now pretty well, and it is worth a good deal to see his face, it is so brimful of life and sunshine and gladness.

*January 22d.*—Eddy is fifteen months today. He has eight teeth, his hair begins to curl, and his face is full of smiles. He says "There 'tis," quite plainly, and *tries* to say "baby." He is very cunning and interesting; will tell what the cow says, and call the cat. He and Annie play horse, as he wants to be in motion perpetually. He takes down the hearth-brush and tries to push up the latch of the nursery door, in order to get down-stairs, and will trot across the room with the poker, in order to drive his ball from under the sofa.

*March 22d.*—Eddy is seventeen months old

He keeps us all laughing as we watch his funny little capers. While Annie was sick, he would come in and punch her with a stick thrust through the bars of the crib, in order to make her get up and play with him, and if I was not careful, would hurt her head. After she got able to sit up, he did not know what to make of it, and would try to pull her from my lap, making signs to have her put into her crib. He now calls her "Addie," and his nurse "Mardet," and says a number of words. Whatever A. does, he does, and he is all stir and noise and life and smiles; fat, and as well as one could expect him to be, while he has four big teeth swelling his gums to the size of walnuts. He is a dear little boy to us.

*April 22d.*—All his first four double teeth have pricked through, and he is feeling rather unwell, and looks pale and somewhat thin. He has begun, however, to walk out, and enjoys it with all his heart. He does not say as many words as A. did at his age, but has quite a number—" baby—kitty, pretty," etc. He wears the sack and hat A. has worn all winter, and his foot is larger than hers, so she has *his* cast-off shoes and stockings. He is very affectionate still, and when I go into the nursery runs to throw his arms round my neck, and will hang on me, with his little soft face pressing closer and closer to mine, as long as I will let him!

Early in June, with the hope of improving my health, I went with A. to Newark. As it was necessary for me to stay longer than I intended, and they, as well as myself, all longed to see Eddy, we persuaded his father to come on with him and his nurse. He stayed two weeks and then returned, taking both the children, hoping by this means to give me a better opportunity to recover my strength. During my continued absence from home, his father wrote of Eddy: "He is finely this morning; it would have done your heart good to hear him *laugh and scream* while M.

was at breakfast; running and riding on my back. How I love the little fellow!" and again: "He makes great dependence on spending M.'s meal-times with me; is very affectionate, and we have grand sport running from parlor to study, throwing beans at each other, and making believe eat the wall, at which he fairly beats me. When I ask him for mamma and Annie, he makes great ado, and points vehemently to the front door."

During their visit to Newark, the children took the whooping cough, and on hearing that this was the case I hastened home. Eddy had it very lightly and only whooped once. But as long as it lasted, he was rather feeble, and required much care and attention. When we removed to Newark, in October, he was looking delicate in consequence of his cough, but soon began to recruit, and shortly became, as we thought, the very picture of health. He never had had so brilliant a color in his life, as during this winter, and he was in such fine spirits and enjoyed everything so much, that he was like sunshine wherever he went. Every night he and A. were brought to the parlor, and their father had a little frolic with them. Eddy enjoyed this wonderfully; and his shouts of merriment still ring in my ears. Whatever he enjoyed, he enjoyed very heartily. His nurse was sick for three weeks in the early part of this winter, and he then came to the table with us, and used to take his walks out with A. and myself. During these walks he was full of pretty little talk, not one word of which can I now recall. But there is one record in the journal, for this winter.

*January*, 1851.—Eddy is a dear little boy, very gentle, very loving, and at times, beautiful. He is learning to talk very fast; and says such little sentences as these: "My man sick." "I see Annie." "My man up 'tairs." "Annie gone away," etc. He has invented names for his favorite toys; his ninepins are "ni-men-ees"; his houses, "shootoos," and his night-dress is a "*dan*-down." He loves to hug and kiss, and when he is well is very sweet and pleasant and docile. He has had two little conflicts with me, in which I have, with ease, come off conqueror, and I think has but little self-will. He is neat and orderly, and won't go to bed till he has picked up and put away all his playthings.

Books and ninepins are his idols. There is one trait in his character which I ought to mention. A year ago, when he and A. had their suppers in the nursery, he would not taste his own, until he had fixed a cushion for her to sit upon, and seen her lifted into her chair. Ever since he could put two words together, no matter what he had given him, he *always* says, "*An-nie*, too"; and often won't taste a morsel till he sees her provided also. He will save a part of what he has given him in her absence, until he sees her again, when he will run to give it to her. The other day I came in with a little toy-horse for him; and before he would touch it, he said: "Buy Annie one, too!" And when he had drawn it across the room, he said, "Now, *Annie* drag it," with such infinite sweetness, that she could not help throwing her arms round him and kissing him.

One day of this winter Miss E. M—— met him out walking with his nurse with a very disconsolate air; and on inquiring what was the matter, he told her he wanted a "little boy-baby." She went home and made one for him, with which he was highly delighted. When she gave it to him he would not kiss her for it, but seemed shy and in a hurry to run to exhibit it to his nurse, but afterwards he repented, and said: "I wish Mit Miller would tum again, so I could kiss her." He gave his baby the name of "Charley," and it was the last toy he ever noticed.

His father used to tell him that by and

by he should have all his books, and would take perfect delight in asking him, "Who's going to have papa's books?" and hearing him say in the prettiest manner, "*I* am; but I shall give *Annie* some"—which was the invariable addition. He was the most unselfish child I ever saw.

Early in May he had the measles, but so lightly that I did not think it worth while to ask the doctor to see him. Annie had been quite sick with them, and I knew just what to do. He was more fretful than was usual with him in sickness, and both he and A. got well rather slowly, owing, I thought, to our removal to New York, during which we had to turn them off a good deal. Eddy was so regular in his habits, and had such an aversion to confusion and disorder, that all the process of moving and getting to rights, annoyed him; and when we came to this house, said repeatedly: "I don't like this house *at all!*" But as soon as we subsided into a quiet and regular life, he became very happy, and enjoyed greatly his large, airy nursery.

In June we procured a waitress, whose name was Margaret, on which by way of distinguishing them, he began to address his nurse as "*my* Marget." He took no fancy to this new Maggy, but felt it his duty to pray for her from the night of her arrival until he could pray no longer. "God bless Marget," he had been in the habit of saying; but now it was "God bless *two* Margets." His little cousin Annie P. visited us after this; he became very fond of her, and prayed for her with his sister: "God bless two Annies." As long as she stayed with us he called *our* Annie "*my* Annie," and it sounded so prettily to hear him say, "My Annie, will you tome play with me?" "My Annie! I will dive you half my blocks."

One day in the season of strawberries, we had some on the dinner-table, and A. had her share of them. As we were leaving the table, her father selected and offered to her a large one, and merely to try her, I said: "Don't you want papa to eat that himself?" She is far from being a selfish child; but until this year, we had never allowed her to eat fruit. She hesitated; on which her father said: "You want papa to eat it, don't you?" She smiled, but still hesitated, and after amusing ourselves a little about it, we let her eat it herself. I then proposed to make an experiment of like nature on Eddy. We were not in the habit of giving him fruit, but he was as fond of it as other children, and the beautiful red strawberry always attracted his eyes. His father selected three very fine ones, and we proceeded to the nursery. I called him to see what we had brought for him, and put a large pin into his hand, telling him to eat them. He was highly pleased, put his pin into the largest, and was just conveying it to his mouth, when I said: "Don't you want to give that nice large one to dear papa?" With his bright, quick smile, he instantly ran and held it to his papa's lips. And we had some difficulty in convincing him that his father had already eaten enough, downstairs. He then devoured it himself, with great gusto, but offered the second to me; on my refusing over and over again to take it, he ran to his nurse and urged it upon her, and on her positive and repeated refusal to accept it, ate that also. "Now," said he, taking up the last one, "I want *Annie* to have this one." And she could hardly induce him not to force it into her mouth.

## III.

*Sunshine still—Baby Talk and Ways—Shadows of coming Trouble.*

To sleep, to sleep, my baby dear,
Mamma is nigh thee, do not fear;
Close those bright eyes, and lay away
Those dainty limbs, so glad all day.
      Hush! do not cry,
      But listen to my lullaby.

No bird had e'er so sweet a nest,
In which to hide away and rest;
Now nestle in it soft and warm,
Nothing shall come to do thee harm.
      Hush! do not cry,
      But listen to my lullaby.

Thou sweetest one! thou darling child!
Thou blossom fair and undefiled!
Our household joy! our sunbeam bright!
Love shall thy cradle be all night.
      Hush! do not cry,
      But listen to my lullaby.

## III.

NOW follows the last record I made in his journal.

*July*, 1851.—Eddy is now two years and nine months old. He is quite large, and has grown almost too fast during the last month. As to talking, he now keeps up a perfect chatter; and I can see indications of humor, which in so young a child are amusing enough. He is as precise and orderly as ever, but is growing more and more roguish, and takes a real boy's delight in teasing Annie. He will keep kissing the back of her neck when she is busy and doesn't want to be disturbed; or will touch her with one finger and then run off and hide, laughing all the way.

Last Sunday I was holding him at the window to keep him from falling out, as he was eager to see people returning from church; and he kept saying things to make them look up and laugh, until I was ashamed to be seen. One sentence poured out after another, as fast as his tongue could fly. "Oh, do see those two *t*olored women! Their faces are black and dirty!" "Oh, do see that little dear *t*urly-head!" "You gemplen! there is a happy land in eternity!" "What's that lady *d*ot in her hand? A doll! no, a live baby!" and so on, with a dozen speeches I can't remember, the fun of which was in the manner rather than in the matter. He is as restless as he well can be; there is no holding him in one's lap, as a pet, or telling of stories, or singing; if you sing one thing he calls for something else till you yield the field. When he has been naughty, he does not scream and kick, but stands still till he recovers his good humor. It takes a good deal to vex him, but very little to wound his feelings. A sharp word grieves him exceedingly, and calls forth a shower of silent tears.

On the 21st of this month we all went to Rockaway to visit Mr. and Mrs. B—— We had moved about so much of late that Eddy seemed to think we were now about taking final leave of New York, for on reaching the hotel at Jamaica, where we were obliged to spend the night, he said: "This is our home." He enjoyed this visit at Rockaway very much, pronouncing the sand on the shore "*clean* dirt," and taking great delight in playing with it. We had him bathed twice; he did not like it at all, and when he saw his nurse afterwards go into the water, he cried till she came out again. He said they were going to drown her, and received her, on her return to the shore, with every demonstration of relief and satisfaction. He was as brown as a nut when we returned home.

On the 1st of August his father left home, intending to be absent five or six weeks. As the children stood at the window, seeing him off, I was amused at their characteristic remarks. A. said, "Papa will *never* come back again. I am afraid we shall never see him any more." "Oh, yes, he will," returned Eddy; "he will come back, *certainly*." And during his papa's whole absence, his frequent, "Oh, I don't *like* to have papa gone!" "I wish papa would not stay so long!" was invariably followed with, "But he will come home soon." He begged all summer to be allowed to go to church, but I was afraid he would not sit still; one Sunday, however, he coaxed so prettily, that I consented to let him go and sit with his nurse in the gallery, whence he could be removed, should he begin to disturb the congregation. He was so elated by this permission, that I could hardly make him listen while I charged him to be a good boy. As I was putting on his sack, I said to M. that if he fell asleep, I wished her to take it off. "Ho!" said he, "I sha'n't go to sleep! Christ don't have rocking-chairs in His house!" In this vivacious state he set off, followed by our loving eyes till he was out of sight. Soon after service commenced, I heard him laugh loud and begin to play with a parasol; M. then took him out. He was very sorry he had behaved so, and often said he would not do so again if I would try him once more.

About this time I got for him a pair of little white pantaloons, and made a French shirt to wear with them. He was delighted, and said, "Now I am a little gentleman"; and was so pleased that I let him lay aside his frocks sooner than I had intended. His father was pleased too, on his return from his journey, to find his little boy in boy's garments, and made him run up and down that he might see how cunning he looked. I was about going to Newark when this change was made in his dress, and Eddy asked if he might go too, and let his grandmother see his pantaloons, especially the *pockets*. This was on the

11th of August. He spent the day very happily with his little cousins, and I was glad I had consented to his going.

I stayed until the next Saturday with A., when she became quite unwell, and I returned with her. Eddy was grieved to see her sick, and wanted to hang round and kiss her continually, and often said: "Mamma, why don't you *say* something to my Annie?" as if he thought I might comfort her with loving words. About this time he said to me, "Mamma, if I die you must put me out in the 'treet." I asked why? He was lying in bed, and looked up to the wall, as he answered: "Christ wouldn't like to have to break through that wall to get me." At another time, as he sat at his little table, he said, as if to himself, "When I go to heaven, I shall take hold of mamma's hand." He now began to enjoy hearing Bible stories, and particularly about the man to whom Christ gave eyes, and the restoration of the withered hand. He had tried for a year nearly, to learn hymns, and would say: "Tinkle, tinkle, little 'tar"; and "*Fusser* little children to tum unto me"—with indescribable sweetness.

His aunt Mary from New Orleans came to visit us, with her children, in September. On the 29th, we took them all to Barnum's Museum. I took Eddy under my own special care, and enjoyed *his* enjoyment of all he saw. He laughed very heartily at the "Happy Family," and his shouts of pleasure filled the room—but he could not be happy unless Annie were near. "I want my Annie to see this!" he would exclaim at every new object that attracted his eye. His father weighed all the children; Eddy weighed 29 lbs.

His uncle Charles was here during most of August and September, and played with him a good deal, carrying him on his shoulders and lifting him up to touch the wall. When he went back to Portland,

Eddy cried, but soon consoled himself in his usual style. "But he will come back soon." He missed his aunt and little cousins, too, and prayed for them every night; particularly for Una, who had played with him a good deal.

On the 18th of October Mrs. Randall and her sister, Miss Deborah S., old and dear New Bedford friends, came. During their visit, he appeared well and bright, and they often spoke of his being such a *happy* child, and of his amusing himself so much, and making so little trouble. He used at this time to run round to kiss us all, as soon as family prayers were over, with such a sun-shiny face. Before they left us, early in November, I observed one morning at prayers that he looked pale, and spoke of it. I felt more uneasy than seemed rational. He was getting two teeth, however, and I concluded they were the occasion of his looking ill. But he never appeared well to me again. His complexion changed, he had quite a bad cough, and began to be nervous and irritable. I was exceedingly disappointed. His uncles Henry and George arrived on the 6th of November from California, and I had thought so much of the pleasure they would take in him, and he in them! But he was shy, and avoided them all he could, and generally was not willing they should even kiss him.

About the middle of the month I sent for the doctor. He said there appeared to be some gastric derangement, prescribed for him, and at the end of a week he seemed better; but he was very nervous, and did not act like himself. I spoke of this to the doctor, who said he perhaps needed to return to a more generous diet, and that we had better begin to give him meat once a day—especially chicken, perhaps oysters. I sent out instantly for a few oysters, as it was too late in the day to cook chicken, and he enjoyed them. He always called them "little birds." The next day I gave him a bit of chicken, which he also enjoyed, and made arrangements for him to have chicken-broth every day for a week. I had promised to spend Thanksgiving at Williamstown if he were well enough to make it safe for me to leave him. His uncles did not wish to go without me, and thought Eddy did not need me at all, as he was playing about as usual and out of the doctor's hands. I never left home so reluctantly, however. I felt extreme uneasiness about Eddy; more than I could account for.

We left at 5 P.M., November 25, and returned in just a week from that night. Eddy was awake when I hastened into the nursery to see him, though it was midnight, and sitting up in bed. He seemed glad to see me again, and gave me one of his sweetest smiles of welcome. On seeing him next morning, however, I was disappointed. He did not appear to have gained anything during my absence, though his nurse said his appetite had been good, and that he had enjoyed his little Thanksgiving dinner very much. I thought he would perhaps recover his strength as soon as he could begin regularly to take the air, and had him taken down-stairs that morning, directing M. to allow him, with certain restrictions, to return to his usual diet.

I was very unwell myself at this time, and when lying on the couch in the nursery had leisure to watch him as he played about the room. He struck me as much changed. In a few minutes he would get tired of his toys, and sigh, as if fatigued; now and then he would come and climb upon the couch and lie by my side, on my arm, with one little hand and arm thrown over my neck. This was not natural in a child so full of vivacity as he had been; and as I thus lay with him like an infant in my embrace, tears often filled my eyes. If he observed it, he would draw closer, pat my face with his hand, and say, "Poor mamma! *dear* mamma!" over and over again. More than once I observed him to laugh and cry at once in a hysterical manner, very painful to witness. He would now only sit in just such a chair, and get into bed just so, and have his little table just so. One day some food was brought up for A. on a dining-room plate. On seeing it, he said, "*I* don't eat off such a nice plate, *at all*." I told him he should do so if he wished. He said, "Is there a *lady* on that plate?" and on my telling him there was not, he said, "I can't eat unless there is a lady on my plate." There was a picture of one on the kitchen plates.

On the 19th of December the Rev. Mr. P——was here. On hearing of it, Eddy said he wanted to see him. As he took now so little interest in anything that would cost him an effort, I was surprised, but told Annie to lead him down to the parlor. On reaching it, they found Mr. P. was not there, and they then went up to the study. I heard their father's joyous greeting as he opened his door for them, and how he welcomed Eddy, in particular, with a perfect shower of kisses and caresses. This was the last time the dear child's own feet ever took him there; but his father afterwards frequently carried him up in his arms and amused him with pictures, especially with what Eddy called the "*bear books.*"

Thinking our late dinners not proper for him in his now feeble state, I had one prepared for him at twelve, and he enjoyed this change. At times he would be as bright and playful as ever. When I played with A. and himself, for instance, he would run and laugh and shout as he used to do—the difference being that he now soon flagged as if fatigued. His nervousness and irritability increased from day to day, and he wanted to be amused instead of amusing himself, and to sit a great deal in M.'s or my own lap. One morning Ellen told him she was going to make a little pie for his dinner, but on his next appearance in the kitchen told him she had let it burn all up in the oven, and that she felt *dreadfully* about it. "Never mind, Ellie," said he, "mamma does not like to have me eat pie; but when I *get well* I shall have as many as I want."

One day in the early autumn I said, by way of amusing the children, that I thought God would send us a little baby by and by. They were even more delighted than I expected; and A., looking up, said, "I shall be all the time looking up till I see it come flying down from heaven." Eddy looked up, and said, "*I* shall too." "Oh, you are such a little boy, you don't even know which way to look towards heaven," said A., who fancied his eyes turned in a wrong direction. After this, I do not think a day passed in which some allusion was not made to this longed-for baby. No matter how fretful and unwell he might be, it invariably would bring a happy smile to his face, if I said to him, "When my little baby comes, you shall take it in your arms." I made use of this idea to divert him when he was restless.

Once, when talking about it, he asked me some question, I forget what, which made me take him up in my lap and tell him something about his own suffering babyhood. "Where was my Marget then?" he asked. I told him she had not come here, but was taking care of another baby. "Well," said he, with that expression of humor about the mouth which had so often amused me, "I was *t*ying for her all that time—*that* was what I was *t*ying for!" Again he came to me, and said, with this same expression, "What *t*olor are my eyes?" He knew perfectly well, as he did the color of everything. I smiled, and said, "Why, you little rogue, you know they are black." "Well,

I hope my little brother-boy's eyes will be black, then; I want him to look just like me."

Sometimes he would leave his play and run to M., and say, "We must be very good to that little baby when it comes. If we are not kind to it, God will take it right back to heaven again"; or, "I shall give my little brother all my toys." Once, on hearing this, I asked if he would give it his nine-pins, this being his favorite toy. After a moment's reflection, he said, "Yes, and all my blocks too." He was very fond of his nurse, and would hardly allow her to leave the room or go anywhere without him, but often said, with great cheerfulness, "When my little brother comes, *I* will sleep with Annie and let *him* sleep with Marget"; and "When we take our journey next summer papa will carry Annie, mamma will carry me, and I will let *my Marget* carry the baby." Although *we* never spoke of the baby as a boy, he always insisted on its being a "brother-boy"; and one day, as if to explain this, said to his nurse: "Marget, little *dirls* like little *dirls* best ; but little boys like little boys best."

I said to M. one day that I was glad I had put Eddy into boy's clothes, as I should want his frocks, etc., for the baby, not supposing he observed what I said. Shortly afterwards, however, on seeing her change her dress on her return from church on Sunday, he asked her *why* she changed it ; and on her replying, "To save it," he said, "Oh, I suppose you are saving it for your little sister," and added that he was saving all his for his little brother. Owing to his playing about less, I could now interest him with stories to more advantage than ever before. He wanted to hear about "the little fly that hadn't any breakfast," over and over and over again. I also read to him from various little books such stories as he could understand.

IV.

*Christmas—Faint Sunbeams amid thickening Shadows—In Doubt and Perplexity.*

So be it; 'tis Thy plan, not mine,
   And being Thine, is good ;
My God, my will shall yield to Thine
   Ere it is understood.

## IV.

I WAS much interested in preparing for Christmas, and promised myself great pleasure in seeing the children hang up their little stockings. They talked about it a good deal, and not realizing that it was the state of his health which made Eddy appear tired of all his toys, I flattered myself that he would enjoy some new ones still more. I said to their father that I wanted to make this Christmas a very happy day to the children, and that we might not all be together on the next. On the 24th Mr. Stearns and Anna were here. I was out with Anna much of the day. On my return, Eddy came to me with a little flag which his uncle had given him; and after they had left us, he ran up and down with it; and as my eyes followed him, I thought he looked happier and brighter, and more like himself than I had seen him for a long time. He kept saying, "*Mr.* Stearns gave me this flag!" and then would correct himself, and say, "I mean my *uncle* Stearns." A dear friend had sent the children some grapes; I asked Eddy if he wanted one, and told him to help himself, as they lay within his reach. Presently I asked him if he would like another, and he said no. As he was *very* fond of them, I was surprised at this, and asked why not? He said he had had one. I told him he might have another, and welcome, on which he said he was afraid it would hurt him, and that he would wait till he got well. I saw that he *longed* for more, notwithstanding, and took him on my lap and gave him several, when, as usual, he returned the seeds and skins. A few days before, an apple was offered me, which I declined, saying I was afraid it would make Eddy want it, to see me eat it. He was then on my lap. "Oh, I don't want any," said he, "because it might make me sick; but when I get well I shall have a whole *basket* full."

While M. was out of the room towards night, he brought his flag to me and climbed into my lap with it, saying, with great animation, "Mamma! when your little baby sees this flag, it will *dance for joy!*" M. then came and lighted a lamp; I was busy, at his request, in rolling up the flag to be put away for the night, and did not observe what he was doing until I heard him cry out that the light hurt his eyes. Knowing but too well what this cry might indicate, I looked at him anxiously, and asked if his head ached. He said it did not, but that M. was a "naughty *d*irl" to let the light shine in his eyes and make *them* ache.

For some time, I think for weeks, his sleep had been restless and disturbed. He would grind his teeth, scream, moan, and talk, from the time he fell asleep until after midnight, when he would be more quiet. I used to dread his bedtime on this account; it was distressing to see such signs of suffering. His nurse was so *sure* he had worms, and said so often that she had seen children suffering with them, give just such tokens of their presence, that I had allowed myself to be somewhat relieved on this point; but only by fits and starts, as it were. On this night he hung up his bag for his presents, and after going to bed, surveyed it with a chuckle of pleasure peculiar to him, and finally fell asleep in this happy mood. I took great delight in arranging his and A.'s presents, and getting them safely into the bags. He enjoyed Christmas as much as I had reason to expect he would, in his state of health, and was busy among his new playthings all day. Miss Bleecker sent him a toy which gratified him extremely. I enjoyed this day myself; it was the first on which I had had *two* children old enough to enjoy a little festival, and Eddy was brighter and better than usual.

After going to bed that night and repeating his prayer, he said to his nurse, "I don't want to be *died*, but I want to be a little angel without being died." I was pleased to hear him say this in his sweet, clear voice; but as soon as he fell asleep he began to moan and throw himself about as usual, and seemed to think some one was getting his toys away. I feared he had eaten too much candy, as he had had a variety in his bag. On asking his nurse, however, she said she had put most of it aside, at his request, and showed me that very little had been eaten. I felt of his head and hands, as I always did the last thing before going to bed, but observed only a very slight degree of unnatural heat in either; still, in contrast with A.'s, they were too dry and warm.

The next morning Miss Bleecker sent for

the children to come in there for a few hours; Annie went, and his nurse soon after took Eddy in, but he was languid and uninterested, and soon asked to be brought home. On his return, feeling very anxious about him, I took him up and began rocking and singing to him, and he soon fell asleep. The rest of the day one cheek was red and the other pale, and I observed this to be the case repeatedly afterwards. He had had for some time little feverish turns, but they were so slight as hardly to be noticeable, nor did they last more than fifteen minutes at any one time. Still, they restrained me from giving him tonics, as I should otherwise have done. He began this week to be disturbed by noise, and said once, as he lay in my arms, "Oh, I *wish* the boys in the street wouldn't make so much noise!" and again, "The boys in the street make more noise than they used to."

On the 29th Mrs. Washburn came in to

invite us to take tea with her. Eddy was going down-stairs as she came in, and she stopped and spoke with him. In the evening she told me she had seen him, and thought him a dear little fellow. I replied that he was not looking like himself, and that I was feeling anxious about him. This was a very mild day, and he asked if he might ride out. Thinking the air would refresh him, I directed M. to take him in an omnibus to the foot of Cortlandt street, and promised him, if this did not fatigue him too much, he should go every day to ride. I should not have allowed him to go had I known the state his poor little head was in; but as he always declared it did not ache, I had allowed my fears concerning it to slumber for a season. He enjoyed his ride down, but on reaching the ferry said that was the way to grandma's, and urged M. to let him go to Newark to see her. On her telling him she could not without mamma's leave, he said no more, but laid his head on her shoulder, and did not lift it again until they reached home. He fell asleep then, and I reproached myself with having sent him so far, and it seems now as if I might have *known* the fatal disease which was fastening itself upon him. But I must remember that most of " his symptoms needed the event to interpret them."

The next day I was out a good deal on business. As I was dressing to go, Eddy asked if he might go with me, and seemed unusually disappointed when I told him I was going too far for his strength. I told M. she might take him a short distance; she did so, and they went as far as the corner of the Bowery and Fourth street. Even this little walk fatigued him, so that she brought him home in her arms. He had taken his last walk on earth, and never went out again until he left this weary, weary world for that in which the weary are at rest. Towards night A. cried a little about a book I had taken from her It worried and grieved him, and he came and stood by my side in an inconvenient position to himself, as he stood on tiptoe to throw one arm around my neck. .

I then took him in my arms and carried him down into the parlor, where I sat down with him on the rug, and asked him if he did not think that bright fire beautiful. I wished to ascertain the effect of light on his eyes. He turned his head away, sighed, and said he did not. I then directed his attention to the solar lamp which had just been lighted. He said he did not like to look at it, that it made his eyes ache, and sighed again. Then looking up at the bright circle on the ceiling above the lamp, he said, "But I think *that* is pretty." He then sat quite silent and abstracted, with his head on my breast, and I missed that incessant little prattle which he always used to keep up if taken to any new place.

The next morning he was quite bright while taking his bath, and said, "How my uncle Henry would laugh to see me in my tub!" He took the sponge, as usual, and wet his head with it. In the course of the day, as he lay in my arms, he asked me to "ride" him to see his uncles, cousin "Eddy *Hocsins*" [Hopkins], etc., reminding me of each one. I had lately amused him in this way as I sat rocking him gently in my lap, and it had gratified him not a little. He often asked when his uncle Henry would come; and once when he did so, M. said, "Why, you wouldn't love him when he was here before." "I would *now*," he said. On this, as well as the preceding morning, we had taken him to the breakfast-table with us. I wished to take the entire care of his diet myself. Feeble as he was, he would not allow me to help him down-stairs, but went by himself. He hardly tasted his food on either of these mornings, and seemed to be lost in thought.

For a week or ten days past he had changed his seat at prayers from M.'s side to my own, and while his father read the Scripture he held my hand. On this morning he called M. to come and sit on his other side and hold his other hand. There was something very touching in his appearance as he thus sat; his little figure, already wasted and languid, looked so helpless, as it were, so anxious for the support love even could not give it. He had taken a fancy within a few weeks to kneel with me at my chair, and would throw one little arm round my neck, while with the other hand he so prettily and seriously covered his eyes. As their heads touched my face as they thus knelt, I observed that Eddy's felt hot when compared with A.'s—just enough so to increase my uneasiness.

On the afternoon of this day, which was the last of the year, Mrs. S—— sent over two little chairs for the children, with the message that the arm-chair was for Eddy and the rocking-chair for A. Before the coverings were removed, Eddy said *he* should like the rocking-chair best. I then told A. how unwell he was, and asked her to let him have his choice. She consented at once, and on examination we found the arm-chair was too high for him and just right for her; so both were suited. He was very much pleased with his, pointed out its peculiarities, rocked in it, and said he would now give his old one to "the baby." Towards night I proposed that these chairs should be placed in the parlor, as they would soon get injured if kept in the nursery. He objected a little at first, but soon went down with his himself, selected a place for it, and put it there with his own hands.

He slept miserably this evening, and threw himself about all over the bed. I went to him several times and asked the question I had already asked scores of times, "*Where* is Eddy sick?" and he gave his usual answer of "I don't know." I offered to bathe his head, but he would not allow it; afterwards, however, he called me to come and comb it, and I did so gently, a long time, hoping to soothe his nerves by this means. Mrs. B—— had sent some New Year's toys for the children, and as he was wide awake and very restless, I let M. exhibit to him one which I thought must certainly attract him. "Take it away! take it away!" he cried out, as if it distressed him to be called upon to admire anything.

# V.

*The Agony of Suspense—"Via Dolorosa"—
Alone with her dying Boy—Cheering him
with Song and Story.*

So be it; I, a child of dust,
　　Will not oppose Thy way;
Move on, mysterious Will; I trust,
　　I love, and will obey.

# V.

ON entering the nursery on New Year's morning, I was struck with his appearance, as he lay in bed; his face being spotted all over. On asking M. about it, she said he had been crying, and that this had occasioned the spots. This did not seem probable to me, for I had never seen anything of this kind on his face before. How little I knew that these were the last tears my darling would ever shed! It occurred to me that as scarlet fever was more or less prevalent, he might have taken it; this would account for most of the symptoms which had made me uneasy. I had always dreaded this fearful disease, but now said to myself, "*Anything* but water on the brain!"—and went down to breakfast really elated, thinking I would now have the doctor see him. I waited until he came to make his New Year's call; he came early, and I asked him up to see Eddy, and told him everything that I thought would throw light upon the case. He said he should not like to prescribe any remedy until he knew the disease; asked if he had had the measles, and said he would come the next day.

I felt more easy, and spent most of the day in the parlor, receiving visitors; as often as I could I ran up to look at Eddy, or take him in my arms. He was very restless, and looked pale; and there was an expression of pain in his eyes. He did not play on this day, but once or twice had some of his toys arranged on a table, where he could look at them. He slept a good deal. Miss Bronson sent him a box of very pretty blocks; he aroused himself on seeing them, and wanted me to spread them out on the table, but did not touch them himself. A., who stood where she could see his face, cried out that he was smiling at them. If so, it was for the last time.

On Saturday, January 3, Dr. B. ordered two grains of calomel, to be followed by magnesia, etc. Eddy had now a very slight, but frequent cough, which seemed to annoy him; every time he coughed he would mention it to M. and then to me. He showed great aversion to noise; if A. moved or sang or read, he would say, "Don't, Annie!" And it was a trial to him to have her even kiss his hand. Sometimes he would not let his nurse hold him, and then he would turn to me; then all of a sudden, would cry out for his Marget. again. He took his powders without objecting, and afterward a great spoonful of rhubarb mixture. He was tortured with constant nausea, and it cost him a great effort to take this large dose; on my promising to tell papa and grandmamma what a good boy he was, he swallowed it cheerfully. He said again on this day: "I do wish my uncle Henry would come." He slept much, and had no appetite.

Early in the morning he asked to sit in his little chair and have his hair cut off; I accordingly cut a good deal from the back of his head; after which, as he seemed tired, I said we would let the rest go till some other time, and then took him up. He was in my arms nearly the whole day, as he would neither lie on the bed or let me take him. . . . . About dusk he manifested great distress, and tore hair from his head by the handful, which I took from his clenched fingers and laid aside. I had now little doubt as to the nature and seat of the disease; I could not restrain a few tears. A. hung round him and said: "Mamma, if Eddy has many more such dreadful pains, I am afraid he will die." When she said this, I supposed him to be asleep; but without opening his eyes, he said quickly: "No, Annie! No, Annie! I sha'n't die." He had another restless night; I came into the nursery repeatedly during the night, unable to sleep myself, and heavy-hearted indeed. He would not allow me to take him, however, and after sitting awhile idle and anxious I would return to bed.

On Sunday morning, January 4, not being able to come himself, Dr. B. sent Doctor W. in his place. We had succeeded in persuading Eddy not to be entirely dressed, as he had been hitherto, and he now lay a little at a time on the bed in his dressing-gown. I told Dr. W. that I thought he had water on the brain; he said he had not, but might have worms, and ordered nothing but a warm bath. . . . About noon, on this day, he rallied for more than an hour; asked for his candies which had been put away on Christmas day, and had them arranged on the table. I told him I thought I might lend him a box to keep them in, he had so many, and he was interested in seeing me look for one. I had two little pink hearts left, or rather a heart and a ring, and told him he might have one of them; he selected one and put it into the box himself.

I then brought a little bottle, into which he had taken pleasure in dropping, one by one, a quantity of tiny sugar-plums; he played in this way a few minutes, I holding the bottle and M. the plums for him. It did seem *so* pleasant to see him amusing himself once more! He talked a great deal all the time, but we do not remember a word he said; it was about his playthings—his usual little prattle. He appeared to sleep most of the afternoon, and when he found us preparing his bath at night, objected to going into his tub, strenuously, but at last consented. He had a very restless night; slept little, and complained of pain in every part of his body; now of his feet and legs, now of his arms and hands, then of his forehead, then of the back of his neck.

On awaking, Monday morning, January 5, he said: "Marget, why didn't I have my own doctor yesterday? What did that other man come here for?" And soon after to me: "Oh, mamma, there have been hairs in my eyes all night, and my teeth ached." His father wanted to carry him about the room in his arms, but he declined. He had wanted the shutters closed the day before, but now asked M. to open them, and she did so. He would not let me hold him much, and was very restless. When the doctor came I told him that Eddy was unable to retain any nourishment; he said I might try ice-cream, and at night apply a mustard plaster to the back of his neck and soak his feet. I sent instantly for the ice-cream, but owing to some misunderstanding failed to procure any. I then went down and mixed a little snow, cream, and sugar together, with the hope that this might possibly tempt his appetite. He took several teaspoonfuls and said it was "*dood.*"

Soon after, as I was sitting with him in his little chair, he said, mournfully, looking towards the window: "I wish I could see leaves on those trees once more." Touched by his manner, and by the thought these words suggested, I could not restrain a few tears; and then said, "Mamma thinks that before the leaves come again upon the trees, her little darling will be where the leaves never fade." I did not expect or wish him to understand this, but A. immediately said, "Mamma means that she thinks you will be in heaven before long." "I don't want to die," he returned. I then said as cheerfully as I could: "Why, you know it is a *great deal* pleasanter in heaven than it is here. There are no old, naked trees there; little boys don't have the headache there; *I* should love dearly to go, if God should say I might." "Yes," said A.; "don't you know how we used to sing about 'that happy land'?" I then began to sing that little hymn beginning:

"Around the throne of God in heaven, ten thousand children stand," till my fainting heart was cheered. The next time he was alone with his nurse, he said: "Marget, shall I ever see the leaves come on those trees?" Not knowing what had passed, she said: "Of course you will." "My mamma said *perhaps* I shouldn't," he returned.

Soon after this he said to me: "Mamma, I must go to the top of the house now." "Oh, no; not to-day, must you?" I said. "Yes, I must go; there is a lady there who has been waiting for me *all day;* she has *dot* something for me." I perceived that his mind was wandering, and again began to sing, in order to soothe him, and he relapsed into a sort of stupor in which he lay some time. He said repeatedly during this day: "Oh, I don't *like* to be sick!" "Oh, I *wish* God would make me get well." Towards night we applied the plaster; we had a good deal of trouble in keeping it on, for this was his restless time of day, and he did not appear to know what he was saying or doing. It drew very well, but gave no relief. He had, if possible, a worse night than the previous one, and would not take a particle of nourishment, though now very feeble from the want of it.

In the morning, January 6, I offered him everything I could think of, but in vain. Not knowing what to do, and seeing him almost fainting with exhaustion, I said, "Does my Eddy want to die?" He said, "No, I don't want to die *at all*." I told him he would certainly die if he neither ate nor drank, and asked if he would not take just one little baby teaspoonful of jelly to please mamma, who would cry very much if he should die. He then consented to my putting a very little into his mouth. Not knowing that it would be safe to do otherwise, I had made this jelly without wine, but with a good deal of lemon-juice, hoping thus to make it palatable. His father was going to Newark, and came in to bid him good-bye, asking if he would send a kiss to grandma. He kissed him, and very soon relapsed into a stupor, in which he lay with his eyes rolled up into his head, when he suddenly started up. I sent M. for some more snow and cream, and he sat without support on my lap while I fed him with it, as he would not allow her to do so. During these five minutes the doctor came in, and was deceived, I suppose, by his appearance. I told him it was a transient exertion of strength, and that he had not noticed anything since the early morning; and now for the first time said to him that I believed there was water on the brain. To this he returned no answer and left the room.

Eddy, in the meantime, had thrown himself back upon my arm, in a stupor again. The moment the doctor had left, M. burst into tears; for myself, I was almost desperate. A long day and a long night, during which we had nothing to do but hang over this failing child. I gave him to his nurse and went into my room, where I walked up and down in a fever of suspense and distress. Already worn with sleepless, anxious nights and restless days, I felt unable to endure the pressure of another day and night of solitary care, nor could I find it easy to say: "Thy will be done!" I said to myself that I was willing to give my child to God; but that this *uncertainty* I should sink under. Then I reflected that even *this* was divinely ordered, and so trying to trust and not be afraid, I returned to my little darling. He looked even more ill as I now saw him in his nurse's arms than when in my own. It was a dreadful day; so stormy without that I did not feel it would be right to send for any friend; so stormy in my heart that it was like a troubled sea.

When his father returned at night, I told

him what a day I had spent; that Eddy had been apparently unconscious ever since noon, and gave no sign of life whatever, save by the gentlest little breathing which I had to listen for with my ear near his mouth. He said he had seen sicker children repeatedly, in his pastoral visits; but if I wished he would go and ask Dr. B. his opinion of the case. I said that his opinion for *that day* was founded on false appearances; that if he considered Eddy in as critical a state as I did, he would have been in again this evening, and that I should not have been surprised to see the poor little boy drop away at almost any moment, his prostration was now so very great. On hearing all this, his father said he should go round and see the doctor, and accordingly did so. Dr. B. said it was a puzzling case; that he had feared that disease of the head was creeping on and establishing itself; but that there might be worms—and that Doctor W. was divided, with himself, between these two points.

Eddy lay all night in this exhausted condition; and on Wednesday morning, January 7, for the first time, did not insist on being dressed. He remained, therefore, in bed, with no pulse at the wrist, but with his eyes wide open. When Dr. B. came in, he put his ear to Eddy's mouth, just as I had done, and said he must as soon as possible have an enema of beef-tea, a wine-glassful every four hours; and that he wished to call in Dr. Johnson, as consulting physician. My own mind had now become calm, and its strugglings were over. I saw what God would have of me, and that He was going to help me through what lay before me.

Soon after the administration of the first enema Eddy revived, and continued to improve in strength all day, but was more and more restless. Mrs. B—— came early in the morning, and offered to send her cradle for his use; he said after she went out, on hearing us talking about it, that he would not lie in a "*c*radle." We tried to hold him, but I thought it must fatigue him more to lie in our arms than on the bed or in a cradle. When it came, which was late in the afternoon, his restlessness was very great, and he did not like it long at a time. In the course of the day he would often sigh, and say: "Oh, *so* tired!" And repeated what he had said before: "I *wish* God would make me get well."

On Thursday, January 8, while M. was at dinner, I knelt by the side of the cradle, rocking it very gently, and he asked me to tell him a story. I asked what about, and he said: "A little boy"; on which I said something like this: "Mamma knows a dear little boy who was very sick. His head ached, and he felt sick all over. God said, 'I must let that little lamb come into my fold; then his head will never ache again, and he will be a very happy little lamb.'" I used the words "little lamb," because he was so fond of them. Often he would run to his nurse with his face full of animation, and say: "Marget! mamma says I am her little lamb!" While I was telling him this story his eyes were fixed intelligently on my face. I then said: "Would you like to know the name of this boy?" With eagerness he said, "Yes; yes, mamma." Taking his dear little hand in mine, and kissing it, I said: "It was Eddy." Just then M. came in, and his attention was diverted, so I said no more.

## VI.

*Still watching and waiting—A parting Kiss—
The Good-bye—The* MASTER *comes!—"It
is* WELL *with the Child"*

## TO MY DYING EDDY.

*January* 16*th.*

Blest child! Dear child! For thee is Jesus call-
    ing;
And of our household thee—and only thee!
Oh, hasten hence! to His embraces hasten!
    Sweet shall thy rest and safe thy shelter be.

Thou who unguarded ne'er hast left our threshold,
    Alone must venture now an unknown way;
Yet, fear not! Footprints of an Infant Holy
    Lie on thy path; thou canst not go astray.

## VI.

HE presently asked to be taken up; M. was about doing so, when he said, "No, I want mamma to." I was not able to lift him up, though I could hold him without much difficulty, and M. therefore lifted him for me as usual. He sank into his stupor almost immediately, and continued in this state for about an hour, when he suddenly started up and said he wanted his little table set out. M. rose and got it for him, placing it as near him as possible. "Now bring my chair." This having been done, he said, "Now *hurry* and get my dinner." I told M. she might bring some of the jelly I had made for him, which was in the next room, and his little mug of water; and when this was also done he resisted my attempt to place him in his chair, saying he could get down himself. He could not bear his own weight on his feet, however, and let us help him into his chair, where he sat some minutes feeding himself with a little spoon. There was an expression of anguish in his eyes and an air of stern resolution about him which made it painful to see him exerting himself to such a degree; and yet there was a pleasure in seeing him once more in the old familiar place. I was sorry his father was not at home to see his little sufferer contending so patiently with disease.

Thinking he would probably never take food again, I put away his little spoon in another room. He was now in M.'s lap, and very uneasy; she, too, looked very tired, and for both their sakes I asked him if he would lie on the bed if I would lie by his side. He consented, but soon called M. to lie on his other side, and as she did so, became more restless, and soon told her to get up and lie on the floor. Then, as if fearful he had hurt her feelings, he asked me to give her a pillow, and, to gratify him, I did so, though I knew she was not on the floor. He said many rather incoherent things, and finally told *me* to get up and make room for his Marget. We gratified him in this also, and I then went down to tea. As soon as I had gone, he asked M. to rub the back of his head, and as she did so, cried out, "Rub harder! rub harder! rub *harder!*" till uttering a scream he threw himself across the bed, in a fit.

On going down to tea I had said to M. she could ring the bell if anything happened. She had not the least idea what I meant, but she now flew to the bell and rang it. I screamed out, "Eddy has a fit!" and was in the nursery almost in the twinkling of an eye, his father following me like one distracted, saying, "Remember your life is of more consequence to me than that of a hundred children." In two minutes, thanks to our bathing-room, we had the poor little rigid form in warm water. While in the tub, his cries were fearful, and rent my heart with their strange, unnatural sound; his hands were clenched and his eyes fixed, but there was little convulsive agitation. In eight or ten minutes I had him taken from the water and wrapped in blankets and laid in my arms. I had never seen a child in a fit, and was so agitated that I hardly knew what was best to be done, nor how long it was proper he should remain in the bath. His father had gone for the doctor, who applied a mustard plaster to the pit of his stomach. In about an hour he recovered consciousness, and looked up at me as he would have done if awaking from sleep. Miss Bleecker, for whom I had sent, was here, and said she would spend the night. The doctor gave directions for a blister, and its application to the back of his neck, and ordered one or two more enemas of beef-tea before morning. We now put on the dear child's night-clothes and applied the blister; he appeared to sleep until the blister began to draw, when he cried out at intervals till 5 A.M., "Oh, mamma! my neck! oh, Marget! my neck!" in accents of distress which my ears will ever hear. At this time he had another fit like the first, and was unconscious for about three-quarters of an hour. On recovering, he looked at me with that same intelligent but surprised glance I had seen before.

As soon as it became light, on the morning of the 9th, he raised himself a little and looked round the room, saying, "Where's Annie? I want her." I told him it made her cry so to see him sick that I had put her into papa's bed. He said again, "I *want* her!" and she says now, "Oh, mamma! why *didn't* you call me!" He lay in the cradle all day, most of the time unconscious; his eyes were open and very brilliant. Mrs. S. came early and stayed most of the day. Once Eddy tried to speak, but could not; he then made signs that he had a sore finger and that he wanted a rag on it. He had picked at it until it was quite inflamed.

In the afternoon Dr. B. brought Dr. Johnson, and on their asking him to put out his tongue he did so. On leaving, they directed nothing but wine whey. Dr. B. came again in the evening, and said we might give about two tablespoonfuls every hour from a cup, if he would drink from one. I had asked if it would be safe to take him up, put on clean clothes, and get him more comfortably fixed in a crib Mrs. S. had offered to send over. Dr. B. thought it not only safe, but advisable.

. . . . He was very neat, and dearly loved to have clean clothes on, and after some persuasion, consented readily. But little time as it occupied to make the change, it fatigued him so much that it was two hours from the moment he was taken up before we ventured to put him into the crib. It was so comforting to have him once more in my arms that I was only willing, for his sake, to lay him down.

Louise Shipman came in at this time and offered to spend the night, but as we had made other arrangements, I asked her to come next day instead. She did so, and did not leave us again till all was over. Mrs. Tracy watched this night, and I threw myself on the nursery bed, and made M. do the same, as we both were worn out. I did not sleep, but heard Mrs. T. every hour give Eddy his wine whey and sometimes water. Towards morning he kept saying, as if remonstrating with some one urging it upon him, "I don't *want* any more water"—over and over, from which I perceived that his mind was wandering again.

On going to him Saturday morning, January 10, I observed at once that his countenance had changed, and that he did not see any of us, and feared he was soon to leave us. At seven he was seized with spasms, which affected only one side, and which lasted two hours. When they ceased, he looked tranquil and beautiful beyond description. His eyes were lighted up with the brilliancy lent by this disease, and the very spirit of heaven seemed to look forth from that lovely countenance. We stood around the crib fascinated and soothed, expecting every moment that his sun would go down amid these bright clouds. Contrary to these expectations, however, he lingered on, but as he could not swallow, and began to look extremely worn and exhausted, it was painful to see his heaven-bound spirit still detained and imprisoned here. Mrs. B—— watched with him this night, during which he appeared comfortable, and could take wine whey and water. His head was kept wet, or had a bag of ice applied to it; this refreshed and relieved him evidently.

On Sunday, January 11, he took drinks frequently. I had not left the room since Thursday evening for more than three minutes at a time, fearing he would drop away in my absence. Mr. and Mrs. Bull came in, and Mrs. Smith, who offered to stay then or come at night, and it was arranged that she should spend the night. Oh, how many kind friends now surrounded us! How many friendly acts were performed! How many prayers offered for us and for our little one! May God, who has recorded them all, bless those whom He moved to sympathize with us in our affliction!

At noon, while they were all at dinner or elsewhere, I was left alone with my darling for a few moments, and could not help kissing his unconscious lips. To my utter amazement he looked up and plainly recognized me, and warmly returned my kiss. Then he said, feebly but distinctly, twice, "I want some meat and potatoes." I was transported with joy. I do not think I should have been more delighted if he had risen from the dead once more to recognize me. Oh, it was *such* a comfort to feel again the sweet pressure of those little lips, and to be able to gratify one more wish! Mrs. Wainwright had sent in some calves'-foot jelly and grapes. I was about to put some of the jelly into his mouth when he put forth his little thin hand and took it from me, feeding himself with it eagerly, and as if *starving*. I then asked him if he would have a grape; he said "Yes," in his own sweet way, and he took it from me as he had done with the jelly, returning the skin and seeds as usual. Before they returned to the room he had sunk away again.

Dr. Johnson came in, and was surprised, apparently, at his having asked for food, and said I should by all means give him everything I thought he would fancy. After this, as long as he could swallow, he was fed, just like a little pet robin, with ice-cream, jelly, little bits of sugar, and ice. One night he ate six grapes besides some jelly. About six in the evening, as his father sat by his side with the dear little hand in his own, Eddy looked up and recognized him, and spoke to him twice, but in so faint a whisper that we could not understand what he said. Shortly after this he began to sink rapidly, and we all sat in silence around him, expecting every moment would be his last. We sat thus for five hours, during which a little pulsation in the neck was the only indication that life still lingered. As it approached midnight, his father stopped the noisy clock, whose loud tones we all dreaded. At this moment Eddy partly turned over, pointing with his hand to his neck. We had not been able to dress his blister since Friday night, as he had been lying on his back ever since; but now, as he remained inclining to one side, it was dressed without disturbing him. He was so relieved by the dressing on this occasion that he put his hand up to his nurse's neck, just as he did in health when he loved her best, and so fell sweetly asleep.

The next day, January 12, his uncle Stearns and aunt Anna spent with us. He had another sinking turn in the course of it, but rallied again, and took jelly and grapes which a friend brought for him.

All day on Tuesday, January 13, he lay in a lethargy; could hardly swallow, and had a more flushed and feverish appearance than he had ever done.

At half-past two on Wednesday morning, January 14, slight spasms came on; they continued for some hours, and increased his exhaustion. He took little nourishment after this, as it was difficult for him to swallow; a teaspoonful of water or a bit of ice, and once a very little icecream. I went to sleep in my own room on Wednesday and Thursday nights, as I was now fearful of doing wrong in neglecting proper care of my health for the sake of the baby. I made M., too, try to get some sleep in another room, as she looked greatly worn, and was suffering much in parting with her loving charge.

On Friday, January 16, his little weary sighs became more profound, and as the day advanced, more like groans, but appeared to indicate extreme fatigue rather than severe pain. Towards night his breathing became quick and laborious, and between seven and eight, slight spasms agitated his little feeble frame. He uttered cries of distress for a few minutes, when they ceased, and his loving and gentle spirit ascended to that world where thousands of holy children, and the blessed company of angels, and our blessed Lord Jesus, I doubt not, joyfully welcomed him. Now, indeed, we were able to say: *It is well with the child!*

"Oh," said the gardener, as he passed

down the garden walk: "who plucked that flower? Who gathered that plant?" His fellow-servant answered: "The MAS-TER!" And the gardener held his peace.

---

(*The following is from a letter of Mrs. Prentiss to her brother Henry, dated January 26, 1852.*)

His father closed his eyes in an agony of weeping; and I threw myself down by his little crib and thanked God that those eyelids, which for a whole week had been open, could now repose in a sleep from which they never need waken. Yes, I was glad that my darling had got away from this weary world, and that I had now a little angel in heaven. I had said that no hands but mine should fit him for the grave, but God knows how to break us in to His will when He sees best to do so. I was alarmed for the safety of my yet unseen baby which had given no sign of life since the night of dear Eddy's fit, and let them persuade me to sit by, while M. and Louise did what little there was to be done. Then we knelt down, and George prayed with such faith and fervor that at last a few tears refreshed my tired eyes, which I feared would never weep again. The funeral was on Monday. Dr. Skinner officiated, and the choir came over and sung, "Thy will be done," most delightfully. It was like cold water to thirsty souls. This was all we had to say or could say. The little body lies almost within a stone's throw of us, for the present, and the little spirit is all about us, whispering words of comfort and cheering us even in our saddest hours.

I need not try to tell you how much we miss those dear little feet, how much we talk of all his pretty ways, how at times it seems as if we heard his voice on the stairs. Every hour we feel more and more that he is gone and gone forever; and every hour the sharp pang presses harder and harder, until our hearts die within us. . . . . We have been *loaded* with kindness from every direction, and our people have manifested the most hearty sympathy. Louise Shipman endeared herself to us very much, and we feel most grateful to her. Mrs. Bull was here day and night, and watched every other night for a week; and I have had some of the most comforting little notes sent in. I used to think I could never endure to lose a child, but you see how it is. God does carry us through anything He pleases.

# VII.

*Little Bessie—A Moment here; then gone forever—The Mother's Lament.*

Jesus, I turn to Thee! oh, let me hide
        Within Thy breast;
Refuge and shelter, peace and grace provide,
        And needed rest.

For in the mazes of a troublous hour
        I make my way;
Oh, come to me! Thou hast the will, the power,
        Be mine alway!

## VII.

OUR darling Eddy died on the 16th of January. From that time my health was very feeble, and it was a weary and painful thing to bear the baby he had so often spoken of. She was born on the 17th of April. I was too feeble to have any care of her; never had her in my arms but twice; once the day before she died, and once while she was dying. I never saw her little feet. She was a beautiful little creature, with a great quantity of dark hair, and very dark blue eyes. The nurse had to keep her in another room on account of my illness. When she was a month old she brought her to me one afternoon. "This child is perfectly beautiful," said she. "To-morrow I mean to dress her up and have her likeness taken."

I asked her to get me up in bed and let me take her a minute. She objected, and I urged her a good deal, till at last she consented. The moment I took her I was struck by her unearthly, absolutely angelic expression, and not being strong enough to help it, burst out crying, bitterly, and cried all the afternoon, while I was struggling to give her up.

Her father was at Newark. When he came home at dark, I told him I was sure that baby was going to die. He laughed at me; said my weak health made me fancy it, and asked the nurse if the child was not well. She said she was perfectly well. My presentiment remained, however, in full force, and the first thing next morning I asked Margaret to go and see how baby was. She came back, saying: "She is very well. She lies there on the bed scolding to herself." I cried out to have her instantly brought to me; M. refused, saying the nurse would be displeased.

But my anxieties were excited by her use of the word "scolding," as I knew no baby a month old did anything of that sort, and insisted on its being brought to me. The instant I touched it I felt its head to be of a burning heat, and sent for the nurse at once. When she came, I said: "This child is *very sick*." "Yes," she said; "but I wanted you to have your breakfast first. At one o'clock in the night I found a little swelling. I do not know what it is, but the child is certainly very sick." On examination I knew it was erysipelas. "Don't say that!" said the nurse, and burst into tears. I made them get me up and partly dress me, as I was so excited I could not stay in bed. The doctor came at 10 o'clock; he expressed no anxiety, but prescribed for her, and George went out to get what he ordered.

The nurse brought her to me at 11 o'clock, and begged me to observe that the spot had turned black. I knew at once that this was fearful, fatal disease, and entreated George to go and tell the doctor. He went to please me, though he saw no need of it, and gave a wrong message to the doctor, to the effect that the swelling was increasing, to which the doctor replied that it naturally would do so. The little creature whose moans Margaret had termed *scolding*, now was heard all over that floor; every breath a moan that tore my heart in pieces. I begged to have her brought to me, but the nurse sent word she was too sick to be moved. I then begged the nurse to come and tell me exactly what she thought of her, but she said she would not leave her. I then crawled on my hands and knees into the room, being unable then and for a long time after to bear my weight on my feet. What a scene our nursery presented! Everything upset and tossed about; medicines here and there on the floor, a fire like a fiery furnace, and Miss H. sitting hopelessly and with falling tears, with the baby on a pillow in her lap. All its boasted beauty gone forever. The sight was appalling, and its moans heart-rending. George came and got me back to my sofa, and said he felt as if he should jump out of the window every time he heard that dreadful sound. He had to go out, and made me promise not to try to go to the nursery till his return. I foolishly promised. Mrs. White called, and I told her I was going to lose my baby; she was very kind and went in to see it, but I believe expressed no opinion as to its state. But she repeated an expression which I repeated to myself many times that day, and have repeated thousands of times since, "*God never makes a mistake.*"

Margaret went, soon after she left, to see how the poor little creature was, and did not come back. Hour passed after hour and no one came. I lay racked with cruel torture, bitterly regretting my promise to George, listening to those moans till I was nearly wild. Then, in a frenzy of despair, I pulled myself over to my bureau where I had arranged the dainty little garments my darling was to wear, and which I had promised myself so much pleasure in seeing her wear. I took out everything she would need for her burial with a sort of wild pleasure, in doing for her one little service, where I had hoped to render so many. She it was whom we expected to fill our lost Eddy's vacant place; we thought we had *had* our sorrow and that now our joy had come. As I lay back exhausted with those garments on my breast, Louisa Shipman[1] opened the door. One glance at my piteous face, for oh, how glad I was to see her! made her burst into tears before she knew what she was crying for.

"Oh, go bring me news from my poor dying baby!" I almost screamed as she

---

[1] Her cousin, whose sudden death occurred under the same roof in October of the next year.

approached me; "and see, here are her grave-clothes." "Oh, Lizzy, have you gone crazy?" cried she, with a fresh burst of tears. I besought her to go, told her how my promise bound me, made her listen to those terrible sounds which two doors could not shut out.

As she left the room she met Dr. B., and they went to the nursery together. She soon came back, quiet and composed, but very sorrowful.

"Yes, she is dying," said she; "the doctor says so. She will not live an hour."

.... At last, we heard the sound of George's key. Louisa ran to call him. I crawled once more to the nursery, and snatched my baby in fierce triumph from the nurse. At least once I would hold my child, and nobody should prevent me. George, pale as death, baptized her as I held her in my trembling arms; there were a few more of those terrible, never-to-be-forgotten sounds, and at 7 o'clock we were once more left with only one child. A short, sharp conflict, and our baby was gone.

Dr. B. came in later and said the whole thing was to him like a thunderclap, as it was to her poor father. To me it followed closely on the presentiment that in some measure prepared me for it. Here I sit with empty hands. I have had the little coffin in my arms, but my baby's face could not be seen, so rudely had death marred it. Empty hands, empty hands, a worn-out, exhausted body, and unutterable longings to flee from a world that has had for me so many sharp experiences. God help me, my baby, my baby; God help me, my little lost Eddy.

## BESSIE.

They have put away the cradle forever out of sight;
They have folded up and laid away the little garments white;
They have ransacked every drawer; every cupboard they've laid bare;
Lest mine eye perchance should fall on what my baby used to wear!

But my sorrow and amazement—they have left *them* as they lay—
No tender, thoughtful hand has yet folded these away;
My rooms restored to order, look as they did before,
But will the old look haply to my heart return once more?

I fancied, little daughter, thou hadst flown to my embrace,
To fill with thy sweet presence, thy brother's empty place;
I said, "I've *had* my sorrow! Now welcome to my joy!
He sends this precious baby who took my only boy!"

Why flee that place, my darling? why didst thou but alight
A moment there, bright vision! then take thy speedy flight?
Was it not warm with tenderness, not rich in love and prayer;
And sacred to his memory who used to nestle there?

Alas! alas! my baby. I loved, I loved thee so!
How eagerly, how thankfully thou surely didst not
    know;
How could that tiny coffin attract thine infant eye?
Why not like other little ones within thy cradle
    lie?

Dear Lord, have pity on me! oh, see my idle hands!
See how my crib stands empty, how my cradle va-
    cant stands;
Of my little ones forsaken, hast Thou aught for me
    to do?
What shall I turn to now? oh, what path shall I
    pursue?

Thou knowest, oh, my Father, what work I love the
    best;
Thou only knowest *how* I clasp my children to my
    breast!
Yet Thou hast taken from me the task I fancied
    Thine,
Thy hand it has bereft me of the treasures I thought
    mine.

Oh, let me not distrust Thee in this hour of my dis-
    tress;
Close, closer to Thy side in my sorrow let me press.
What I know not now *Thou* knowest! On that
    rock I plant my feet;
Oh, blessed Lord, I thank Thee for this refuge, sure
    and sweet.

## MY NURSERY. 1852.

I thought that prattling boys and girls
  Would fill this empty room;
That my rich heart would gather flowers
  From childhood's opening bloom.

One child and two green graves are mine,
  This is God's gift to me;
A bleeding, fainting, broken heart—
  This is my gift to Thee.

# VIII.

*Sorrow blossoming into Sympathy—Letters to an old Schoolmate, written in 1854–6.*

Oh, that this heart with grief so well acquainted,
  Might be a fountain rich and sweet and full
For all the weary that have fall'n and fainted
  In life's parched desert, thirsty, sorrowful!

## VIII.

### To Mrs. M. C. H. C.

NEW YORK, *March* 25, 1854.

How could you say, my dear Carrie, that I don't like long letters! I only wish yours had been twice as long, and that you had told me more about yourself and your little ones — the one here, and the one *there!* Knowing that you have a child where my own two darlings have gone, and thinking that they who never met on earth, are perhaps meeting there, seems to draw me nearer to you than ever. How gladly I would spend days in talking with you over all the way in which the Lord has led us since we parted nine eventful years ago! I can not but think that bereavement of little children is one of our Father's chosen methods of best teaching us lessons of which we are ignorant, and without which few are fit to live. For how few, how very few parents, but know what it means to lay away in the cold earth the little form so tenderly cared for and shielded up to that hour! For myself I feel that I have only *begun* to learn the truths my afflictions were sent to teach me; it makes my heart ache to think how little real good they have done me, and how ignorant and blind I still am. Yet, I can truly say that I feel myself a favored mother, to have been permitted to send two of my children away from my own poor training, my mistakes and follies, to the very bosom of the Good Shepherd. Of those two I may feel assured that they will never sin against God; never be guilty of any of my infirmities, or ever taste the bitter fruits of iniquity. How many comforts we have in such sorrows as ours! What blessedness in the certainty that it is well with our children; *well* beyond our conception: *well* forever and ever.

I feel that you have had a great addition to your affliction in the fact of your husband's absence and utter inability perfectly to share it, at a distance as he was, and if I understand it, of his never having seen his first-born son. But doubtless this trying feature of your lot has its own peculiar work to perform, and will bring its own peculiar blessing. I much wonder that I was so long ignorant of the deaths of your brother and your child; but about that time we went into the country, where we saw only the city papers. I assure you, dear Carrie, you have my warmest love and sympathy. If it were possible, I would go to Portland this summer, and at one time I did think quite seriously of going there for some months. But I could not make up my mind to be separated so long from my husband, except in case of need. Should the cholera make its appearance here, I may yet be driven away. I *hope* you are not going to California, for though I may never see you, I like to feel it not impossible. We ought, both of us, to be wiser and better than we were when we parted.

Thank you for your interest in my little books, with which I am much gratified. I would not have you think little Susy a picture of my A., though many seem to regard it so. Unconsciously I suppose I made them not unlike, yet there is hardly a word of literal truth in the whole book. That about the burned fingers is, and some other little things which related to other children; for instance, Hatty Linton, who is a real child. I only tried to make the story true to nature. The other book[1] I do long to have doing good. I never had such desires about anything in my life; and I never sat down to write without first praying that I might not be suffered to write anything that would do harm, and that, on the contrary, I might be taught to say what would do good. And

---

[1] *The Flower of the Family.*

it has been a great comfort to me that every word of praise I ever have received from others concerning it has been, "*It will do good*," and this I have had from so many sources that amid much trial and sickness ever since its publication, I have had rays of sunshine creeping in now and then to cheer and sustain me. Ill health of the peculiar kind under which I suffer is very depressing; it disposes me to write bitter things against myself, and to think myself a useless cumberer of the ground, so that I really *need* the counter stimulus of an approving word from those I love. Oh, my dear Carrie, how hard it is to live up to one's own ideal! My own book reproached me as I wrote it and reproaches me still, and I often wonder how I *dared* to write for the good of others, when I so poorly practice my own doctrine!

I should love dearly to see your little girl and to have her and my own darling know each other. She is at a sweet age, and I trust will be spared to you. I read to A. all you wrote about "Maymee," to her great delight. Owing to her lonely childhood she is rather too grave and disinclined to go out, or do anything but read; and I was quite amused this morning to hear her ask if I did not wish I had a child less *boyish* than herself, when as a matter of fact, if I changed her habits at all, it would be to those of more life and frolic.

.   .   .   .   .   .   .

I don't know what Louise[1] will say to me if she knows I have written so long a letter to you. I am sure I love her dearly, but I feel a sympathy with you beyond what I can with her, because you are a wife and a mother, which makes it easier

---

[1] Her old Richmond room-mate, Miss A. L. P Lord. Their friendship remained unbroken to the last. Miss Lord died in 1883, greatly beloved by all who knew her.

to write you than her. But I must stop. Do write again soon to

>Your ever affectionate
>>LIZZY.

---

To the same.

NEW YORK, *September* 14, 1854.

MY DEAREST CARRIE:—A few moments ago, after placing my little M. in her cradle, I took up the *Mirror* and read with an aching heart the brief notice of the death of yours. Is it possible, is it indeed possible that you are made childless? Oh, what a world this is! what a world! What would become of us if this were all! I feel distressed for you, my dear friend; I long to fly to you and weep with you; it seems as if I *must* say or do something to comfort you. But God only can help you now, and how thankful I am for a throne of grace and power to commend you, again and again, to Him who doeth all things well. I never realize my own affliction in the loss of my children, as I do when death enters the home of a friend. Then I feel that I *can't have it so;* I can not be willing to know they must suffer so. But why should I think I know better than my Divine Master what is good for me, or good for those I love! Why should I have so little faith, so little submission! Dear Carrie, I trust that in this hour of sorrow you have with you that Presence before which alone sorrow and sighing will flee away. *God* is left; *Christ* is left; sickness, accident, death, can not touch you here. Is not this a blissful thought?

Yesterday a happy mother came to see me, who said with great earnestness that all her eight children were yet spared to her through this sickly season, and that all she wanted was gratitude to God. Another the day before said very nearly the same thing. Yet, sanctified bereavement may be subject of higher and holier gratitude; who knows what the light of eternity will reveal concerning these full households and your empty one? As I sit at my desk my eye is attracted by the row of books before me, and what a comment on life are their very titles! "Songs in the Night," "Light on Little Graves," "The Night of Weeping," "The Death of Little Children," "The Folded Lamb," "The Broken Bud," —these have strayed one by one into my small enclosure, to speak peradventure a word in season unto my weariness. And yet, dear Carrie, this is not all of life. You and I have both tasted some of its highest joys, as well as its deepest sorrows, and it has in reserve for us only just what is best.

If you feel able, do write me all about your dear child. *Everything* will interest me. Since I saw you, another sweet daughter has been lent to me of the Lord. *Lent*, LENT, let me repeat to myself in remembrance of my own sorrow and of yours. She is seven weeks old, and since her birth I have not been without care and trial. My husband's mother has been lying, for weeks, very ill with dysentery; and fatigue and anxiety brought on him a similar attack, which, however, proved less severe, and he is now able to go to see her, though not strong enough to preach. I have been obliged to neglect my baby in my care of these two, and to-day for the first time washed and dressed her. . . . . My trials have made me feel during the last seven weeks that to have no God, is to have nothing, nothing, absolutely nothing. I write in great haste, hardly knowing what; I only want to express my hearty sympathy with you, and to have you know how much nearer and dearer sorrow brings you to my heart. May it bring us both nearer to Christ![1]

---

[1] What a comforter she was! The letter I received from her after the birth of my first-born, I shall never forget. I had taken my three years' old daughter to Chicago, where my husband was going into business. She was a child of remarkable attractiveness and intelligence, and my whole being was wrapped up, as it

To the same.

NEW YORK, *October* 19, 1854.

I read your letter, my dear Carrie, with many tears, and in my heart have answered it twenty times. This morning I do not feel as if I could do anything but commune with some one who knows what sorrow means, for I am oppressed with heavy care. By this time I trust you are established

---

were, in hers. She seemed blessed with abounding health when we left Portland, but almost directly on our reaching C., was taken ill; and among strangers in a strange land her life went out in ten days after our arrival. When all was over, I gave out utterly, and for days lay on my bed, conscious only of a longing to die, and wondering why I could not die. The last words of my darling, as she clung in my arms, had been, "Come after me, mamma, you come after me." This seemed to me my *call*—to follow after my child—and so the dreary days wore on. One morning my husband brought me from the P. O. (into which he had accidentally strayed) a letter from New York, saying, " Whom do you think it can be from?" I grasped it and recognized the handwriting. Then a sudden revulsion of feeling in my weak state brought on a spasm. After a while I read the letter, and oh, how it went to my heart! Lizzy, too, had been be-again in Portland, where I may hope occasionally to see you. How painful was the providence that sent you to a land of strangers to meet affliction! But to your dear little lamb, it was but a brief sojourn there, a sort of entrance-way to the gates of Paradise, and the fold of the Good Shepherd. Blessed will be the day that permits us to go where she has gone. We shall then look back upon life and its dis-

---

reaved; she, too, had suffered (I recalled a precious letter written in 1852, after the death of Eddy and Bessie—a letter whose loss I have bitterly regretted); and I said to myself, "Is it *right* to give myself up to such grief? May it not be God's will that, for my husband's sake, I should *live?*" Well, I was fairly aroused, lifted up, placed upon my feet, and by the grace of God have continued unto this day. This was twenty-nine years ago. Lizzy did not know of my removal from Portland, until she read in the *Christian Mirror* a notice of the death at C. Instantly she was prompted to write, directing simply to Chicago. Our letters were always brought to the house, addressed to the care of Mr. C.'s friend. I have ever felt that there was something providential in my receiving that letter, so full of sympathy, tenderness, pathos! It touched me as if inspired.—[*From a letter of Mrs. C——, dated* PORTLAND, *Oct.* 24, 1883.]

cipline from the right point, and see the "needs be" for it all. When I last wrote you, I did not like to thrust my own sorrow and care upon you in the midst of your overwhelming affliction, and it was selfish in me even to allude to it. Yet I had a sort of feeling that to think of me as rejoicing over a new-born child, while you were mourning the loss of yours, would somewhat jar upon your heart, which would turn for sympathy to the bereaved and not the triumphant mother. . . . . The dear little creature can not raise her head, or support it a second if we raise it for her, and my own opinion, in which I think the doctor now coincides, is that she never will sit upright, much less stand upon her feet. She has emaciated to such a degree that it distresses me to look at her puny face and great bright eyes, and the doctor has ordered a wet-nurse, under whose wing she now sleeps, while I, poor anxious mother, am turned out of my nursery that a stranger may do what I most delighted in doing, and for want of which I feel lost. .... Poor little afflicted darling! My faith has staggered under this new blow, and I blush to tell how hard I find it to say *cheerfully*, "Thy will be done!" But rather than not learn thus to say it, let me go on to suffer as long as I live! Dear Carrie, the hand of the Lord is on us both; let us yield ourselves to His pleasure. Oh, how I do wish, do long to feel an entire, unquestioning submission to Him who pities while He afflicts me!

I feel much for you and think of you every day, praying that the Lord will refine you in the furnace, and so make you more and more meet for His service here, and His presence hereafter. I do trust He comforts you with His presence now, and that you enjoy that of which I now and then catch a blissful glimpse: the sweetness of submission. I can almost fancy that my little Eddy has taken your little Maymee by the hand and led her to the bosom of Jesus. How strange that our children, even our little infants, have seen Him in His glory, whom we are only yet longing for and struggling towards! A struggle indeed it is to me; I am so little in faith, so strong in will, so determined to seek enjoyment away from God. How good He is to condescend to go on year after year, correcting, restraining, teaching us, if haply we will at last give up striving against Him, and yield ourselves to His will! Oh, may He hasten on that blessed day when we shall know no will but His! Dear Carrie, do write often to me: tell me what new thoughts and feelings this sorrow is stirring in your heart; how you spend the time that used to be your child's, and how you speed on your pilgrimage towards that better country whither we are bound. I can not tell you how I feel for you, nor how much I think of you in your lonely hours.

As ever, affectionately yours,

LIZZY.

To the same.

NEW YORK, *February* 4, 1856.

MY DEAR CARRIE:—If I had been sure anything could be said to soothe or relieve you, I should have answered your letter as soon as it was received. But if submission to God's will is what you need for your solace (and I think it is), this is His gift; and He alone can bestow it. Human sympathy and human aid are useless here. Our sorrows are hard enough to bear when borne in unquestioning assent and patience. They must be insupportable when yielded to only as to the inevitable. I have found it very useful in studying my heavenly Father's dealings with me, to ask myself how I would have my child demean herself when under my discipline. Everything of docility, patience, humility, and repentance I require or desire to see in her, He has more right and reason to require from me. He does not want me to ask questions about the mode or time of chastisement, or to struggle with Him when I see the blow coming. He wants me to *submit*. He wants me even to *choose* to be smitten, to thank Him for it with tenderness and contrition, owning it was what I needed and deserved. . . . . *Penitence* comes before submission, and penitence is God's gift; and He is just as willing to grant that as any other of His mercies. When God gave you your sweet little Maymee, He had already ordained that you should keep her only a little while. He sent you to Chicago. He arranged that great aggravation of your affliction, that she should die in a strange land. So you have nothing to do with the question, whether it was wise to go there or not. I took my little Eddy on no journey; he was smitten down at home, surrounded by watch and care. Should I say, "Oh, if I had only taken him away he would have lived!" Such thoughts only torture. They do no good, but sour and embitter the heart already wounded and in need of *solace* rather than aggravation.

And the solace is at hand. God, my Father—my Father who loves me—He has afflicted me; and He makes no mistakes. I have asked Him a thousand times to wean me from this world, and He is answering my prayers. Shall I dispute with Him about His methods? Shall I pretend to know a better way than His infinite wisdom has planned? Oh, my dear Carrie, how often have I walked my room, struggling after the sweet peace and comfort to be found in such thoughts; for, do not for a moment fancy that because I venture to write to you on this subject I have already attained that entire, unfaltering submission, towards which I aim. All I have attained is a great *longing* for it. Sometimes I walk up and down for hours, chafed and torn by the wild beast that rages in my soul, refusing to yield, refusing to be comforted. But I look upon myself at such times as a grievous sinner, and there *are* moments when I can see afar off in the distance, sweet peace and holy submission which shall one day be mine. Oh, let us study our blessed Master's will more and more, till the time comes when we shall learn to count our *mercies* and be silent concerning our sorrows, and shall ask nothing, care for nothing, but to be like Him whose name we bear.

Since I received your letter, we have been greatly moved by a new alarm concerning our dear little daughter. She is now eighteen months old, a sweet age, and we had begun to feel that she might yet enjoy life and help us to enjoy it. She was suddenly taken ill a few nights ago; and lay about twelve hours at the very door of death. The doctor gave us no hope, supposing her to be dying when he came in, and only suggesting that she *might* get through the night. She was quite insensible through the whole, and so nearly gone that her little hands were cold, purple, and stiff. It was a very dreary night. The suddenness of the blow made it startling. Five minutes before she became insensible she was playing peep, and appearing unusually bright and well. Her little blue frock and white apron were lying in her basket just as they were taken off a few minutes before, and it seemed to me I *must* see her in them once more; and my heart ached so for poor A., already bereft of her playmates, and whose love for her little sister is so tender and thoughtful. God spared her, is still sparing her; but at any moment she is likely to be snatched away. Her father feels, as I do, that while the suspense is very hard to bear, every week she lives will be something to remember and enjoy, after she is gone. She is very, very dear to us.

Eddy's little sayings still comfort and are precious to us. We rejoice that we had him three years. Life looks more and more to me like a weary pilgrimage which I am making towards a *home*. I pray God it may always seem so, and that I may forever turn my back on the world and set my face towards Him. Prosperity I begin to dread more than adversity.

"Nearer, my God, to Thee! Nearer to Thee!
E'en though it be a *cross* that raiseth me."

"The Folded Lamb" is the history of a very remarkable little boy, three years old, who died in England. My copy is lent, and I fear lost, or I would send it to you. It would not afford you any *special* comfort, but it is always some solace to a bereaved mother to read about other sweet children, likewise "folded" by the Good Shepherd. He was the most wonderful child I ever heard of. If it will not frighten you to own a Unitarian book, there is one called "Christian Consolations," by Rev. A. P. Peabody, that I think you would find very profitable. I see nothing, or next to nothing, Unitarian in it, while it is *full* of rich, holy experience. One sermon, on "Contingent Events and Providence," touches your case exactly. As to my last little book, I do not suppose you would care anything about it, as it is for little children of eight years. I began another Susy book, but can not do much when so restless, though what I can do is a pleasant resource. If I could cry, I do not think I should write books. But there must be some vent to the activity of brain affliction creates. I should love to see your little Emma. Count your mercies, dear Carrie. What would you do with your *time*, if she did not occupy it? As to Maymee, you know you have not lost her; she is only gone home first, and is waiting; and as Mr. Peabody suggests, *praying* for you there. I have written a long letter, and hope to get a long answer.

With best love, as ever,<br>
Lizzy.

# IX.

*The bright Side of Sorrow—Letters written in 1858–9 and 1866.*

Come unto me, my kindred ! I enfold you
  In an embrace to sufferers only known ;
Close to this heart I tenderly will hold you,
  Suppress no sigh, keep back no tear, no groan.

## IX.

### To Mrs. S. H.

NEW YORK, *January* 20, 1858.

MY DEAR COUSIN:—I have just heard, with great pain, of the death of your dear little boy, and most heartily wish I could say or do something to comfort you. There is, indeed, not much that the tenderest sympathy can do in such affliction as yours, and all ordinary sources of consolation are a painful mockery to the breaking heart. I know it by my own experience; it did me no good to hear people say, "Your child is better off; he might have lived to give you great pain"—for I felt it to be equally true that he might have lived to give me great joy, and that my intense love for him might have made even this weary world a happy home to him. But the simple thought, "*God* has done this; He, who never makes a mistake, has done this"; has it not infinite consolation?

Faith grows strong when great demands are made upon it, and yours truly needs strength, for I do feel that you are sorely smitten. You have your prayers for entire sanctification very painfully answered. But besides the rest the soul finds in just submitting to God's will, there is comfort in knowing that this will is not arbitrary; that the blow may do for us what smiles and gifts never did and never can do. I look with a certain joy on the afflicted child of God, because I know he will have to run to Christ for refuge, and that he will find what he seeks. This is truly a sorrowful world; everybody is tried and tempted and afflicted. How few parents there are who never lost a child! And is it true, is it really true, that the mother who has never known this sorrow, this incurable sorrow, is the mother most to be envied? Do not disappointment and sorrow bear the best fruit?

I know this world never can seem to you as it did before you lost your precious boy; but then think how many, many times you have prayed to be weaned from it. All the Christian needs to help him to bear its trials and losses is a quiet submission to God's will, and a holy courage to endure the pain. Pain I know there must be; no manner of consolation can help that; and when the mind is once convinced of this, and sits patiently down *content* to suffer, or, what is better, rises up cheerfully, though still suffering, the battle is half won. Some one has said she would not be the only unchastened child in her Father's house, if she could; I doubt not you can and do say so too, and that if a wish could recall your dear child, you would not breathe the wish. Oh, how good God is not to give us over to our own way; not to tempt us with too great prosperity; not to grant us our request and send leanness into our souls! I trust and pray, my dear cousin, that He will be very near you now and evermore, giving you such communion with Himself, such peace in believing, such hope of heaven, such sweet submission as are better than ten sons.

I fear I have not said much to comfort you, though I did long to do so; but I know you will accept the wish. Give my love to Mary. She is afflicted in your affliction, I know; but I know, too, that she is one who understands the blessed uses of sorrow and pain.

Yours affectionately,<br>Lizzy.

Mr. P. joins me in every expression of sympathy; and as to the bright side of sorrow, he feels just as I do.

To Mrs. R. K. M.

MONTREUX, *October* 24, 1858.

MY DEAR COUSIN:—What was my grief and pain on taking up the paper, which had been lying round unread for more than a week, to see the notice of the death of your dear little Katie. I read and re-read it, hoping to find, in my selfishness, that it was somebody else's Katie and not yours. I was thinking of you, when I took up the paper, and saying to myself what a long letter I was going to write; but now I feel little heart to write, and you will feel no heart to read a word. Now I realize that there is an ocean between us which not only forbids my flying to see you, but which will for months, perhaps, keep me in ignorance of your state beyond the one bare sad fact which a newspaper has cruelly told me. Dear Hatty, my heart aches for you. That little, bright, sweet face is vividly before me. I know your motherly heart, your anxious temper, and how many trials and sorrows you have already passed through, and tremble lest this blow should quite crush you; and I can not help fearing, that whatever disease snatched her from you, may have assailed the other children also.

This is, indeed, a weary world; and at times when I think of losing my children, I almost triumph in the thought of the heart-sickness, the sorrow, and the conflict they would escape by an early death. But this is not the Christian source of consolation, for at best it is a partial and fitful one. The real solace, the true refuge, I do not doubt you have found, for God does not deal such blows as that under which you are weeping without giving grace and strength to bear them. I often used to wonder how a devoted mother ever lived through the loss of a child, bone of her bone and flesh of her flesh; and I never knew, till I learned the sorrow myself, what secret springs of holy peace and joy He could make it afford. It is, indeed, such a joy and peace as the world knows nothing about, and must needs be mixed with tears and groans as long as we dwell here upon earth. Dear little Katie! happy little Katie! she never will know what this hard world can do to us! She never can know the anguish of remorse or the pangs of a heart out of harmony with itself! Her sunny little life knew nothing about clouds and darkness, and never can. I long to learn every particular about her, and if you do not feel able to write, I hope dear Mary will. How glad I am that you have her faithful heart to lean on in your affliction.

We have taken rooms here, and are keeping house in a pleasant situation near the lake of Geneva, but neither George or myself is well enough to thoroughly enjoy our comforts or our advantages. I see now that he did not stop working any too soon, and that a little delay would have been fatal.

---

To the same.

MONTREUX, *January* 13, 1859.

MY POOR, DARLING HATTY:— I have just received dear Mary's letter, which has made my heart ache for you, and I hardly feel as if I could wait for a letter to go all the way to New York before you can hear how I long to do something, or say something, to comfort you. Oh, what a dreadful world this is, and how happy are your three blessed little ones to have left its sins and sorrows forever behind them! There are times when the burden of life seems too hard to bear, and yet we must go struggling and toiling on, dragging it on with us as best we can. Dear little Rufie! So full of health and beauty! It did seem as if he could not be sick and die! I know what it is to be left with an only child, and all the torture and solicitude of having only one left. But it is true, as George said when we finished reading Mary's letter, that losing a baby a month old is not like giving up such a child as Rufie. God only can give you strength to endure all He has laid upon you; and one source of *earthly* comfort lies open to every broken and bruised heart, which we are perhaps too apt to forget. It is the avoidance of comparisons—the not allowing ourselves to cast one envying glance on other households where sickness and sorrow seem to be almost unknown. If we only can wait till the end we shall see all these mysteries explained; why you should bear children only to lose them with tenfold the anguish the bearing cost you, and why many a mother sees her table surrounded with happy faces, and not one vacant place.

"Soon and forever
The breaking of day

Shall drive all the night-clouds
  Of sorrow away.
We'll see as we're seen
  And learn the deep meaning
Of things that have been,
  When tears and when fears
And when death shall be never,
  Christians with Christ shall be
Soon, and forever."

When I think of all your many trials and afflictions, dear Hatty, how great is the sum of them! And knowing as well as I do all the sweet uses of sorrow, if it were left to me or any earthly friend who loves you to say whether you should ever have another, how we should exclaim and protest against it. And yet how much better God loves you than we do, and how well He knew, when He gave you those dear children, what He was going to do with them and with you. Notwithstanding all He knew you would suffer, He who is very pitiful and of tender mercy let the blow fall. It is a mystery—but a mystery of love — just as all the painful remedies you used for dear little Katie and Rufie would have seemed to them if they could have reasoned about it. "How strange," little Rufie might have said, "if my mother loves me that she gives me medicines that make me so sick!" Oh, dear Hatty, why can we not have more faith? with it we might bear any and every thing! I know it, I see it; but my faith is like a grain of mustard-seed. The least thing sets me to crying out: "What a miserable sinner I must be since God finds it needful so to harass and disappoint and weary me!" when I ought rather to exclaim: "How my blessed Master proves His love for me, a sinner, in not leaving me to the temptations of worldly felicity!"

But if we do see through a glass, darkly, now, it will not always be so. "Soon, and forever," dear Hatty, you will see "face to face"; you will fall down and worship Him who took away little Eddie, Katie, and Rufie, and look back on all your sufferings with the smile of one who has fought the fight, whose battle is ended, and whose victory is won. I do not doubt that even this world may yet afford you some joys and alleviations, for all is not lost; but it never can seem a real home to one who has so often experienced its tribulations as you have. Your only deep and abiding and satisfying happiness must be in God—in trying to live for Him, and in doing and *suffering* His will. May He comfort you as no earthly friend can even try to do, and grant you His peace.

Dear little M., how her childhood has been clouded! Tell her we all love her, and wish we could have her here a little while to tell her so. I am sure she will always be a good child when she remembers that three little angels are watching and praying for her.

The mail that brought Mary's letter, also announced the death of my dear friend,

Mrs. Wainwright, whose loss to me is irreparable, for she was like *a mother* to me. The news came like a thunderclap. I do not know that I ever doubted seeing her again; she had lived through such a long and dangerous illness since we knew her that I fancied her life sure for many years. At any rate I loved her most heartily, and her death makes me tremble when letters come in lest I hear of another loss.

---

To Mrs. M. R. B.

DORSET, *August* 26, 1866.

MY DEAR MRS. B.:—I have been lying on the bed trying to get a little rest before writing you, but my eyes keep filling with tears and will not let me sleep. Dear, darling little Johnnie! All the wealth of affection lavished on him could not keep him away from his real home! I have been thinking with what acclamations we all welcomed him when he lighted down upon us, and of the yet more wondrous joy with which he has been met on the threshold of heaven. How could we have failed to foresee that this pure and spiritual little creature was sent here but for a brief mission, and must inevitably be recalled when his errand was done. For whether we ever know it or not, God knows that this little brief life had a ministry of its own, and that a far-reaching one. I almost envy him, that "he has so easily won his crown, while we must go on fighting for ours." But for you and for you all how sorry, how sorry I am, that you are passing through the weariness and painfulness of a new sorrow, which will revive every one of the past, and make you tremble for the precious things still left you. I am sure I need not say that I pray for you with all my heart, that God would comfort you and keep you. He *can;* and no human sympathy is of much avail. You have been longing and yearning for more perfect union to Christ, and He has perhaps chosen to answer your prayers in this way—painful now and very hard to bear, but afterward it may yield the peaceable fruits of righteousness. How often we cry—

> "Nearer, my God, to Thee! Nearer to Thee,
> E'en tho' it be a cross that raiseth me!"

and then when He takes us at our word, how we shudder and shrink from the very suffering we have invoked.

You are still very rich in children, who will do all they can to comfort you. But this is a great blow for them with their keen sensibilities, and you will feel their sorrow as well as your own. Give my love to them, every one; give my dear little G. a special kiss for me; how I should love to see that sunny head moving about, as we did last summer! I dare not weary you with a longer letter, though I could go on writing all night. Annie sends a great deal of love to you and to all the children. Remember me to your husband, who I know will deeply feel this sorrow, and believe me

Most affectionately yours,

E. PRENTISS.

### OH, DARLING LITTLE BABY.

Oh, darling little baby,
How glad we are you've come!
And now we'll bid you welcome,
We'll sing you welcome home.
We'll love you dearly, baby,
We'll love you night and day—
And Jesus, too, will love you
And keep all harm away.
We'll love, we'll love,
Yes, love, love, love.

You are so pure,
You are so dear,
We're all so glad that you are here,
We're all, we're all so glad that you are here.

Oh, darling baby brother,
We're glad that you are here,
And all your little cooings
Are music to our ear;

We long to have you with us,
Within our happy band,
To kiss and to caress you
And touch your little hand.
We love, we love,
Yes, love, love, love.

You are so pure,
You are so dear,
We're all so glad that you are here,
We're all, we're all so glad that you are here.[1]

---

[1] These lines were written by Mrs. Prentiss after the birth of our little Johnnie. Nine little voices were trained by her daughter A., and the lines were sung under my window just before the setting of the sun, when he was but a few days old. To me the music seemed as from the spirit land, welcoming our darling child. One short year, and he was called to that land, verifying her own words:

"That child will be a saint."

*November* 5, 1879.                              M. R. B.

## X.

*Witnessing for Christ as Healer of the broken-hearted—Letters written in 1870-2—"The Mother"—"Is it well with the Child?"—"Is it well with thee?"*

Dear Lord, my heart was but a willful thing,
Strong in its strength, and ever on the wing;
It needed mastership, and Thou hast claimed it,
It needed taming, and Thy hand has tamed it.
Now, gentle, peaceful, harmless as a dove,
It lives as erst it lived its life, in love;
Love to all living things that Thou hast made,
A love that is all sunshine without shade.
Thy fair, green earth is dotted as with flowers,
With little human souls, and blissful hours
I spend in blessèd ministries to them.
Ah, many a flower I gather, many a gem!
        And I have Thee!

## X.

To Mrs. F. F.

NEW YORK, *October* 19, 1870.

MY DEAR MRS. F.:—I deeply appreciate the Christian kindness that prompted you to write me in the midst of your sorrow. I was prepared for the sad news by a dream, only last night. I fancied myself seeing your dear little boy lying very restlessly on his bed, and proposing to carry him about in my arms to relieve him. He made no objection, and I walked up and down with him a long, long time, when some one of the family took him from me. Instantly his face was illumined by a wondrous smile of delight that he was to leave the arms of a stranger and go to those familiar to him; such a smile, that when I awoke this morning, I said to myself, "Eddie F. has gone to the arms of his Saviour, and gone gladly." You can imagine how your letter, an hour or two later, touched me.

But you have better consolations than dreams can give: the belief that your child will develop without spot or wrinkle or any such thing, into the perfect likeness of Christ, and in your own submission to the unerring will of God. I sometimes think that patient sufferers suffer most; they make less outcry than others, but the grief that has little vent wears sorely.

> "Grace does not steel the faithful heart,
> That it should feel no ill."

And you have many a pang yet before you. It must be so very hard to see twin children part company, to have their paths diverge so soon. But the shadow of death will not always rest on your home; you will emerge from its obscurity into such a light as they who have never sorrowed can not know. We never know, or begin to know, the great Heart that loves us best, till we throw ourselves upon it in the hour of our despair. Friends say and do all they can for us, but they do not know what we suffer or what we need; but Christ, who formed, has penetrated the depths of the mother's heart. He pours in the wine and the oil that no human hand possesses, and "as one whom his mother comforteth, so will He comfort you."

You know, perhaps, that I once had a little Eddy; three months after his death my Bessie went; then came the far greater pain of seeing my poor M. a constant invalid for seven years. *Wave after wave;* and yet I have lived to thank God for it all, and to see that He never was so good to me as when He seemed most severe. Thus I trust and believe it will be with you and your husband. Meanwhile, while the peaceable fruits are growing and ripening, may

God help you through the grievous time that must pass; a grievous time, in which you have my warm sympathy; I know, only too well, all about it.

> "I know my griefs, but then my consolations,
> My joys, and my immortal hopes I know"—

joys unknown to the prosperous, hopes that spring from seed long buried in the dust.

I shall read your books with great interest, I am sure, and who knows how God means to prepare you for future usefulness along the path of pain?

"Every branch that beareth fruit, He purgeth it, that it may bring forth more fruit."

With kindest regards to Mr. F.,
    I am affectionately yours,

            E. PRENTISS.

What an epitaph your boy's own words would be, "It is beautiful to be dead!"

To the same.

NEW YORK, *November* 30, 1870.

MY DEAR MRS. F.:—I thank you so much for your letter about your precious children. I remember them well, all three, and do not wonder that the death of your first-born, coming upon the very footsteps of sorrow, has so nearly crushed you.[1] But what beautiful consolations God gave you by his dying bed—" All safe at God's right hand." What more can the fondest mother's heart ask than such safety as this? I am sure that there will come to you, sooner or later, the sense of Christ's *love* in these repeated sorrows, that in your present bewildered, amazed state you can hardly realize. Let me tell you that I have tried His heart in a long storm, not so very

---

[1] Edward S. died October 14, 1870, aged eight years; Amy Gertrude died November 5, aged one year; Alfred B. died November 12, aged thirteen years.

different from yours, and that I know something of its depths. I will enclose some lines that may give you a moment's light; please not to let them go out of your hands, for no one, not even my husband, has ever seen them.

To go back again to the subject of Christ's love for us, of which I never tire, I want to make you feel that His sufferers are His happiest, most favored disciples. What they learn about Him, His pitifulness, His unwillingness to hurt us, His haste to bind up the very wounds He has inflicted, endear Him so, that at last they burst out into songs of thanksgiving that His "donation of bliss" included in it such donation of pain. Perhaps I have already said to you, for I am fond of saying it,

> "The love of Jesus, what it is
> Only His *sufferers* know."

You ask if your heart will ever be lightsome again? Never again with the lightsomeness that had never known sorrow; but light even to gaiety with the new and higher love born of tribulation. Just as far as a heavenly is superior to even maternal love, will be the elevation and beauty of your new joy—a joy *worth all it costs*. I know what sorrow means; I know it well; but I know, too, what it is to pass out of that prison-house into a peace that passes all understanding; and thousands can say the same. So, my dear, suffering sister, look on and look up; lay hold on Christ with *both your poor, empty hands;* let Him do with you what seemeth Him good; though He slay you, still trust in Him, and I dare, in His name, to promise you a sweeter, better life than you could have known had He left you to drink of the full, dangerous cups of unmingled prosperity. I feel such real and living sympathy with you that I would love to spend weeks by your side trying to bind up your broken heart. But for the gospel of Christ, to hear of such bereavements as yours would appall, would madden one. Yet what a halo surrounds that word "*but*"!

Ever affectionately yours,

E. PRENTISS.

---

*To the same.*

NEW YORK, *January* 8, 1871.

If I need make any apology for writing you so often, it must be this—I can not help it. Having dwelt long in an obscure, oftentimes dark valley, and then passed out into a bright plane of life, I am full of tender yearnings over other souls, and would gladly spend my whole time and strength for them. I long especially to see your feet established on the immovable Rock. It seems to me that God is preparing you for great usefulness by the fiery trial of your faith—"They learn in suffering what they teach in song." Oh, how true this is. Who is so fitted to sing praises to

Christ as he who has learned Him in hours of bereavement, disappointment, and despair?

What you want is to let your intellect go overboard, if need be, and to take what God gives just as a little child takes it, without money and without price. Faith is His, unbelief ours. No process of reasoning can soothe a mother's empty, aching heart, or bring Christ into it to fill up all that great waste room. But faith can; and faith is His gift; a gift to be won by prayer—prayer persistent, patient, determined; prayer that will take no denial; prayer that if it goes away one day unsatisfied, keeps on saying, " Well, there's to-morrow and to-morrow and to-morrow; God may wait to be gracious, and I can wait to receive, but receive I must and will." This is what the Bible means when it says, " The kingdom of heaven suffereth violence, and the violent take it by force." It does not say the eager, the impatient take it by force, but the violent—they who declare, "I will not let Thee go except Thou bless me." This is all heart, not head work. Do I know what I am talking about? Yes, I do; but my intellect is of no use to me when my heart is breaking. I must get down on my knees and own that I am less than nothing; seek *God*, not joy; *consent* to suffer, not cry for relief. And how transcendently good He is when He brings me down to that low place and there shows me that that self-renouncing, self-despairing spot is just the one where He will stoop to meet me!

My dear friend, don't let this great tragedy of sorrow fail to do *everything* for you. It is a dreadful thing to lose children; but a *lost sorrow* is the most fearful experience life can bring. I feel this so strongly that I could go on writing all day. It has been said that the intent of sorrow is to "toss us on to God's promises." Alas, these waves too often toss us away out to sea, where neither sun nor stars appear for many days. I pray earnestly that it may not be so with you.

---

To Mrs. F. G.

DORSET, *August* 1, 1872.

MY DEAR MRS. G.:—We learn from the papers how sorely you are afflicted, and sympathize with you most truly in this irreparable loss. I told Mr. Prentiss I was going to write you, and he cut out your address and put it in my "Daily Food" this morning, in the midst of the hurry of starting off on a journey. As I took up the little book, where for *thirty-seven years* I have been wont to resort for consolation, I was struck with the selection for July 27 —a day that to you will always be memorable, but not always one of unmixed sorrow. I can not forbear quoting them:

"God is our refuge and strength, a very present help in trouble."—PSALM xlvi. 1.

In the darkest dispensations,
  Doth my faithful Lord appear
With His richest consolations,
  To reanimate and cheer;
Sweet affliction, sweet affliction,
  Thus to bring my Saviour near.

"Therefore will not we fear, though the earth be removed, and though the mountains be carried into the midst of the sea."—PSALM xlvi. 2.

To us mothers the loss of a child is indeed like the earth being moved, and I know how you must be suffering. But such a sorrow as this is better than to be passed by and left to unbroken earthly joy, and I believe you will kiss the Father's rod, hurt though it does, and find the only consolation there is in saying, "Thy will be done!" I know no other, but it *is* a consolation, a soul-satisfying one. I wish I had seen your dear baby; but if I had, it would not deepen my sympathy, which springs rather from what I know the poor human heart to be, than from my knowledge that he was so fine a child. This summer has been one of slaughter of the innocents; many and many a heart is bleeding like yours, but has none of the precious promises to sustain and cheer it, as you have.

Mr. P. left messages of love and sympathy for you and your husband.

Affectionately yours,<br>
E. P.

To Mrs. P. S.

DORSET, *August* 25, 1870.

MY DEAR MRS. S.:—I know how little words can do for such a sorrow as yours, yet can not help expressing my most heartfelt sympathy with you in it. You are indeed sorely smitten in having that beautiful boy snatched from you without warning; so sorely, that those who love you must share in your sufferings. May God—who only, of those who love you, could have dared visit you with so wholly unexpected, so terrible a blow — make your darling boy such a minister of heavenly grace and benediction to your soul, as to become associated with a joy with which no stranger may intermeddle. That He *can* do this I have not the shadow of a doubt. Meanwhile, thousands of prayers are ascending for you and for your husband that will help you through the overwhelming days and nights that must come: otherwise, how could your often-bereaved hearts bear on and not utterly sink beneath the waves? "The way to peace," says one who knows the way, "lies through a greater, a warmer, a more tender, a more personal love to God"; this is surely a sweet way to peace, and it has been traversed by many lacerated feet that have come back to tell the story, and to testify, that when the very foundations of the earth seemed giving way, *He* remained whom no accident could snatch away, no chance ever change. Your dear boy reached heaven by a very short and easy path. I remember hearing your husband say once, "From home to heaven," and it is beautiful to think how near they are to each other, and how a child's little footsteps can pass out of the one, only to pass right into the genial heart of the other.[1]

But I feel that I am intruding on a grief that can bear little; forgive me if I have in any way jarred upon you, and believe in the deep sympathy of

    Yours warmly and truly,
                E. PRENTISS.

---

[1] The 'beautiful boy' was nine years old. His sudden death is referred to on p. 354 of the memoir of Mrs. Prentiss. A touching account of him is given in a little volume by Dr. Schaff, entitled *Our Children in Heaven.*

## THE MOTHER.

### I.

As I have seen a mother bend
   With aching, bleeding heart,
O'er lifeless limbs and lifeless face—
   So have I had to part

### II.

With the sweet prattler at my knee,
   The baby from my breast,
And on the lips so cold in death,
   Such farewell kisses prest.

### III.

If I should live a thousand years
   Time's hand can not efface
The features painted on my heart
   Of each belovèd face.

### IV.

If I should bathe in endless seas
   They could not wash away
The memory of these children's forms;—
   How fresh it is to-day.

### V.

Ah, how my grief has taught my heart
   To feel another's woe!
With what a sympathetic pang
   I watch the tear-drops flow!

### VI.

Dear Jesus! must Thou take our lambs,
    Our cherished lambs away?
Thou hast so many, we so few—
    Canst Thou not let them stay?

### VII.

Must the round limbs we love so well,
    Grow stiff and cold in death?
Must all our loveliest flowerets fall
    Before his icy breath?

### VIII.

Nay, Lord, but it is hard, is hard—
    Oh give us faith to see
That grief, not joy, is best for us
    Since it is sent by Thee.

### IX.

And oh, by all our mortal pangs
    Hear Thou the mother's plea—
Be gracious to the darling ones
    We've given back to Thee.

### X.

Let them not miss the mother's love,
    The mother's fond caress;
Gather them to Thy gentle breast
    In faithful tenderness.

### XI.

Oh, lead them into pastures green,
    And unto living springs;
Gather them in Thine arms, and shield
    Beneath Thy blessèd wings.

### XII.

Ah, little reck they that we weep,
    And wring our empty hands;—
Blessèd, thrice blessed are infant feet
    That walk Immanuel's lands!

### XIII.

Blessèd the souls that ne'er shall know
    Of sin the mortal taint,
The hearts that ne'er shall swell with grief
    Or utter a complaint!

### XIV.

Brief pangs for us, long joy for them!
    Thy holy Name we bless,
We could not give them up to Thee,
    Lord, if we loved them less!

---

## "IS IT WELL WITH THE CHILD?"

Yes, it is well! For he has gone from me,
From my poor care, my human fallacy,

Straight to the Master's school, the Shepherd's love.
Blessèd are they whose training is above!
He will grow up in heaven, will never know
The conflicts that attend our life below.
He from his earliest consciousness shall walk
With Christ Himself in glory; he shall talk
With sinless little children, and his ear
No sound discordant, no harsh word shall hear.
Nay, but I have no words with which to tell
How well it is with him—how well, how well!

## "IS IT WELL WITH THEE?"

Yes, it is well! For while with "anguish wild"
I gave to God, who askèd him, my child,
He gave to me strong faith, and peace and joy;
Gave me these blessings when He took my boy.
He gave Himself to me; in boundless grace
Within my deepest depths He took His place;
Made heaven look home-like, made my bleeding heart
In all the grief of other hearts take part;
Brought down my pride, burnt up my hidden dross,
Made me fling down the world and clasp the cross;
Ah, how my inmost soul doth in me swell,
When I declare that all with me is well!

www.ingramcontent.com/pod-product-compliance
Lightning Source LLC
Chambersburg PA
CBHW020833230426
43666CB00007B/1203